AI SEO 2026

Be Found by AI Search –

So You Can Get More Customers

& Make More Money!

by

Christopher Littlestone
www.FoundByAIsearch.com

AI SEO 2026: Be Found by AI Search — So You Can Get More Customers and Make More Money

Paperback – 1st edition
ISBN: 978-1-946373-14-4

Table of Contents

Christopher Littlestone

Preface

Nobody goes to school for SEO.

There's no bachelor's degree in Search Engine Optimization, no diploma that makes you "discoverable." You learn SEO by doing SEO — by failing, adapting, and trying again.

The best SEO professionals are all self-taught. Some are eighteen-year-olds on laptops, building empires from their dorm rooms. Others are fifty-year-old veterans in multimillion-dollar marketing firms. The only real credential is curiosity — and scars.

I'll admit it: for a long time, I didn't get it. I thought good content would speak for itself. I was naive.

My First Failure — I Didn't Learn from It

When I retired from a career in the U.S. Army Special Forces (Green Berets), I wanted to do something meaningful. I had spent my career serving others — protecting the innocent, building stability, making a difference. I wanted to continue that mission in a different way, so my first post-military project was faith-based. It was meant to inspire, to help people grow, to spread light in dark places.

I poured my heart and soul into it. I believed in it. I wrote a book and a daily devotional, and made a web page with hundreds of pages.

But the truth? It failed.

It wasn't because the message was bad or the mission was wrong — it was because nobody saw it.

No matter how much wisdom or passion I invested, the internet didn't care. I was invisible. The world can't listen to what it can't find.

That was the first time I realized something was deeply wrong. I had integrity, purpose, and a good product — but no visibility.

I didn't know it yet, but that failure would become the spark that changed how I looked at the entire digital battlefield. Years later, when I finally understood *why* that project failed, I discovered the hidden system that decides who gets seen and who disappears online.

My Second Failure was a Great Teacher

I pivoted. This time, I wanted to build something closer to my roots — something military, practical, and focused on helping others succeed. So I launched LifeIsASpecialOperation.com.

As a privacy and cybersecurity professional, I didn't want to show my face. I just wanted the ideas to stand on their own. I started making videos — training guides, leadership lessons, mindset development.

At first, it was a hobby. Over time, it grew into something bigger:

- 250+ videos
- 45 million views
- 375,000 subscribers

It was a success by most definitions. And it was meaningful. Every day I'd get messages from young men and women saying, "Thank you. You changed my life."

But I wasn't making real income. The mission was strong, the message was solid, and the feedback was life-changing — but financially, it was flatlining.

During that time, I had a full-time day job serving as a project manager for a Fortune 500 company overseas, and I was also receiving my Army retirement pay. So it was acceptable that I wasn't earning what I could — or should — have been making.

When my corporate contract ended and I finally had the freedom to focus on the business full-time, I made a promise to myself: I would finally learn SEO.

The Academic Detour That Got Me Thinking

While I was on active duty, I earned the privilege of attending Harvard University, where I completed a Master's in Public Administration. Truth be told, after that experience, I never planned to step foot in a classroom again. Academically speaking, once you've been to Harvard, the only way to top it is to return there — or to pursue something not for prestige, but for passion or pure curiosity.

A few years after retiring from the Army, that curiosity came calling. I found myself daydreaming about returning to graduate school — not for a résumé line, but for the simple joy of learning itself.

Eventually, I discovered a Doctorate in Business Administration (DBA) program that felt like a perfect fit. I enrolled, committed, and dove deep into the academic side of business.

My research focused on cybersecurity and privacy perceptions, but what I truly discovered was a new way of thinking. I learned that what separates good businesses from great ones isn't luck, charm, or even vision — it's data. We conducted both qualitative and quantitative research, built models, ran regressions, tested correlations, and performed reliability analyses like Cronbach's alpha until the numbers started to tell stories.

What I took away wasn't a love of statistics — it was a respect for evidence. The best businesses don't make decisions based on hope; they make them based on data.

That mindset became the foundation for how I approach SEO — not from a nerdy or technical angle, but from a practical one. Not as marketing, but as reconnaissance.

Data reveals truth — or at least trends. It tells you what people actually want, where they're looking, and how to meet them halfway.

That same mindset runs through every page of this book.

My Humbling "Now I Get It" Data Moment

I bought a one-month subscription to an SEO analytics platform — the kind that shows you what pages are ranking, who's visiting, and what keywords drive traffic. Out of curiosity, I typed in **Green Beret**.

The results almost made me fall out of my chair.

A random site with no real connection to the Special Operations community — was pulling in an estimated **40,000 visitors per month.**

My site, with its years of real Special Forces experience and content written by an actual Green Beret officer, was getting **forty**. Not 40,000 — but 40.

"What in the world? This is insane," I thought. *"How is that website beating me 1,000 to 1?"*

I had legitimate experience, authentic expertise, and earned authority — but **zero optimization**.

The difference wasn't credibility — it was **structure**. Their page had clean titles, clear metadata, backlinks, and schema markup. Mine had authenticity but no optimization.

That was my moment of truth. And in that moment, I realized something uncomfortable — authority alone doesn't guarantee visibility.

It hit me like a sniper round: the internet doesn't reward truth — it rewards structure. If your expertise isn't formatted correctly, it's invisible.

That was the day I realized I didn't just need to create content — **I needed to engineer discoverability.**

So I went to work. For most people, "learning SEO" means watching a few YouTube tutorials or taking a two-hour paid course. But for an obsessive perfectionist with advanced research skills honed in graduate school, I went all in. I watched every video, read every article, and dissected everything I could find about Search Engine Optimization (SEO).

And the deeper I dug, the clearer it became: **we're standing at a tipping point.**

AI isn't just changing the rules — **it's rewriting the entire game.**

I began to see the AI-enabled internet as a living system — one with its own rules, hierarchies, and invisible power structures. That realization changed everything. SEO stopped feeling like marketing and started feeling like mission planning.

And like every mission I've ever led, success began with two familiar tools: **Anticipate – Mitigate** and **Reverse Engineering**.

Anticipate – Mitigate

After surviving a dangerous career in the Green Berets, I like to frame **"Risk Management"** through the lens of Anticipate – Mitigate: if you can anticipate what's coming, you can mitigate the damage before it arrives. That principle kept people alive on the battlefield — and it applies just as much in business as it does in combat.

I teach **"Anticipate – Mitigate"** everywhere I go. I teach it to Master of Business Administration (MBA) students, and I teach it in all of my security courses. The rule never changes: you must see the threat before it sees you — and then build the countermeasures before it hits.

Right now, one of the biggest unseen threats to most businesses is **AI-driven search**. Artificial intelligence is quietly changing the way people find answers to their problems — and that means it's also changing how they find *you*.

If you don't adapt, if you don't anticipate where this technology is heading, then you'll wake up one morning and realize something chilling: **you've become invisible online.** Your website will still exist, but the machines won't mention it. Your audience won't discover you — not because you did anything wrong, but because the world changed and you didn't.

That's what we're here to prevent, and the best way to do it is to learn to reverse-engineer the system itself.

The purpose of this book is to **anticipate** the shift that's already happening and **mitigate** its impact by taking deliberate action to stay visible. Mitigation means preparing now — strengthening your digital foundation, optimizing your presence, and positioning your business where AI will recognize and recommend you.

Whether you run a multimillion-dollar company or a small-town dental clinic or plumbing service, the principle is the same: if AI search engines can't find you, your customers can't either.

Reverse Engineering

One of the most valuable skills I ever learned as a Special Forces Officer was the art of **reverse engineering** — understanding how a system works so that I could make it work better — for the mission and for the United States.

When I was assigned to help fight the **war on drugs**, I had to study entire networks — the flow of money, logistics, influence, and information — and then deconstruct them to expose their weaknesses. Later, when I arrived at a new **U.S. embassy**, the challenge wasn't kinetic; it was human. I had to quickly analyze the leadership and group dynamics within the embassy, identify the key players and decision-makers, and understand what the important commodities were.

To be effective, I had to **build trust, win hearts and minds**, and earn the permissions and latitude I needed to do my job. The mission always depended on knowing the system better than anyone else — not to manipulate it, but to align with it, to make it work in favor of the mission's success.

AI SEO works the same way. To win here, you have to think like an operator: study the system, understand its incentives, and build strategies that align with its internal logic. That means learning *how AI thinks* — how it reads, classifies, and ranks content. You don't need to trick the system; you need to understand it.

We'll start by reverse-engineering the ecosystem itself: the **history / progress of advertising**, the **evolution of search engines**, and how **machine learning** now drives visibility and trust. Once you understand why SEO existed in the first place — and how AI is rewriting those rules — you'll have the foundation you need to make the system work for *you*.

Visibility isn't luck — it's design. And those who understand the system always win.

The Pivot to AI SEO

Remember at the beginning of the preface when I talked about my first failure?

I had built something I loved — and watched it fail in silence because no one could find it.

Now I finally understood why.

The internet hadn't ignored me — I had ignored the rules of the internet.

Thousands of businesses that once paid a dollar per click are about to get zero — not because their service got worse, but because people have stopped clicking altogether.

They simply ask their favorite AI chatbot for the answer — and trust it. Your ad budget won't matter. Your "sponsored placement" won't save you.

AI SEO is the new battlefield for attention and visibility. Most business owners don't even realize the war has begun.

If you're not optimized for AI, you're going to be left behind — unseen, unheard, and unfound. Just as the internet made the phone book obsolete, AI is now transforming the way we search. Google isn't disappearing — it's evolving. The question is whether your business is evolving with it.

If you're not found by AI, you won't be found at all.

I didn't write this book as a marketer chasing trends — I wrote it as a strategist preparing you for the future.

This book is for real business owners — the ones who work hard, deliver value, and deserve to be found. The entrepreneurs, consultants, and creators who are tired of shouting into the void.

This book is a field manual for the next era of marketing. It's the tactical — not theoretical — version of SEO: practical, disciplined, and brutally effective.

You'll find checklists, prompts, and step-by-step frameworks you can use immediately. I'll show you exactly how to be discovered by the algorithms that now decide what the world sees.

The Cost of Inaction

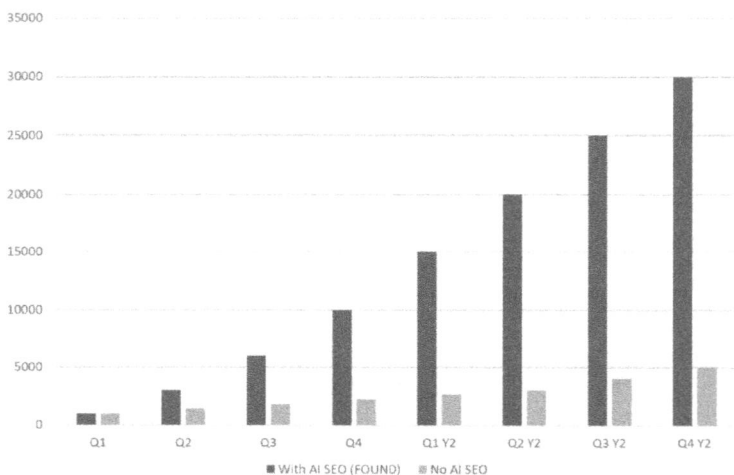

Businesses that adapt to AI search will see exceptional growth in visibility and trust. Those who don't will become invisible. This chart models the projected divergence in organic traffic over the next 24 months.

How This Book Is Organized

I wrote this book intentionally in a conversational tone so you can think through it quickly. You'll notice plenty of open space throughout the pages. That's by design. I want you to use this book like a working manual — jot down your own notes, connections, and ideas about how each concept applies to your business.

This book was written for small-business owners on Main Street — the people who keep America running. The plumber who answers calls at 2 a. m. The car dealer who knows every customer by name. The real estate agent balancing open houses and family dinners. The mechanic who still shakes your hand after an oil change.

A billion-dollar company already has a team of engineers, programmers, and analysts working on their AI SEO strategy. But you — the independent business owner — don't have that luxury. You're busy doing the work that pays the bills. And yet, without realizing it, AI SEO is about to become a critical factor in the survivability of your business.

The **Introduction** lays the groundwork — explaining how AI search engines actually think, how they read content, and how they decide what to show the world. From there, we'll move into the **FOUND Framework** — a five-step process that represents the core of this book and the foundation of everything I teach. It's the same structured system I use to help businesses like yours get found by AI search engines, win more clients, and make more money.

Throughout the book, you'll find **Pro Tips** — short, practical checklists designed specifically for small and medium-sized businesses. These Pro Tips are where strategy becomes action. Each one captures the most important steps you can take immediately to strengthen your online presence and signal credibility to both people and machines.

At the end of the book, I've consolidated every one of those **Pro Tips** into a single chapter. These Pro Tips are organized by our proprietary **FOUND** system (introduced later in this book) — Foundations, Optimization, Utility, Niche Authority, and Data-Driven Improvements. They give you the exact step-by-step process any small or medium-sized business can follow to build visibility, trust, and authority in the age of AI search.

Finally, the book concludes with a consolidated list of the **AI Prompts** mentioned throughout this book. This curated list of ready-to-use AI prompts turns today's most advanced language models into your own personal SEO assistants.

These prompts show you how to use tools like ChatGPT, Gemini, Perplexity, and Bing Copilot as intelligent agents working for your business — helping you research, write, and optimize faster than ever before.

So grab a pen, make notes, and start applying these ideas as you go.

This isn't a textbook — it's a toolkit.

It's not about theory — it's about execution.

And when you finish, you'll have everything you need — a system, a playbook, and a set of AI-powered tools — to make sure that your business is **Found by AI Search**.

A Note to the Reader

Our F. O. U. N. D. methodology isn't magic — it's method.
AI SEO doesn't invent success; it amplifies it.

If you have a solid product, this will magnify your impact.
If your product is weak, this will magnify your weakness.

No amount of optimization can make people love something that isn't good — but great optimization can make a great product unstoppable.

If you've ever felt invisible online, I've been there.
And I built this book so you don't have to stay there.

Because in the AI era, discoverability is survival.
Let's make sure the world can find you.

Introduction: Entering the Era of AI Search

The Name Game

It's always fun to watch the game of *"Name it, claim it."* You know the one — the first person to put a clever label on a trend suddenly becomes the "expert." The right acronym, the right sound bite, and suddenly they're on stage at conferences explaining what everyone else was already thinking.

I saw this long before the AI boom. When I was at Harvard, one of the most famous professors on campus was Joseph Nye — the man who coined the term **"Soft Power."** Even though the U.S. already understood the concept through our instruments of national power — **Diplomatic, Information, Military, and Economic (DIME)** — he captured lightning in a bottle by naming what we'd all been practicing for decades: influence without force. It was so intuitive that we all smiled when we heard it, yet because he had given it a name, it became *the thing*. He was brilliant, of course, but his genius wasn't just the idea — it was the timing and the label. "Soft Power" made him a legend.

I see the same thing happening now in the world of AI-driven search.

Every marketer, agency, and tech pundit is racing to be the first to stamp their initials on what's happening.

AI SEO

– *Artificial Intelligence Search Engine Optimization.* The broad, intuitive term. It bridges the old and the new — traditional SEO principles adapted for AI systems.

AEO

– *Answer Engine Optimization.* Focused on optimizing your content so AI systems generate clear, accurate **answers** that include your brand as a cited source.

GEO

– *Generative Engine Optimization.* Emphasizes the **generative** nature of AI models — that they create new language and synthesize data rather than listing existing pages.

LLM SEO

– *Large Language Model SEO.* A niche label used by developers and data scientists who think in model-specific terms (e. g., "How do we optimize for GPT or Gemini?").

Conversational SEO

– A user-experience term stressing the shift from keyword searches to natural dialogue between human and machine.

AI Discovery Optimization

– A catch-all phrase for being "discoverable" by any intelligent system — not just web search engines, but AI assistants, recommendation feeds, and voice interfaces.

Each name highlights a slightly different angle of the same mission: to make your business *understandable, trustworthy,* and *selectable* by the AI systems people now use to find answers.

2026 will likely be the **vocabulary tipping point** — the year the industry finally agrees on what to call this transformation. As AI chatbots, operating systems, and search tools merge, the buzzwords will settle. Perhaps we'll call it *AEO*. Maybe *AI SEO* will remain the dominant phrase. Or maybe we'll invent an entirely new acronym.

But the truth is — it doesn't really matter.

If my next edition ends up titled **AEO 2030**, the tactics won't change. Whether you call it "answer optimization," "generative visibility," or "semantic marketing," the heart of the process is the same: structure your knowledge so that artificial intelligence can read, interpret, and confidently quote you.

I decided to keep this book title simple and call it **AI SEO** because that phrase instantly tells readers what we're talking about — optimizing for AI-driven search. I could have gone with AEO or GEO, but when you're writing for small business owners who just want to be found, simplicity wins.

So yes, the experts will debate the labels, but the mission stays steady — *clarity over complexity, trust over trend.*

Key Takeaways:

Acronyms will come and go. What endures is the need to be understood.

AI doesn't care what we call the process — it cares whether your message is clear, credible, and structured in a way it can comprehend.

And if history repeats itself, the people who focus on results instead of labels will quietly outperform the ones chasing the next clever acronym.

The Progress of Advertising

Every platform starts the same way: **free, friendly, and full of possibility.**

That's how they draw us in. A new app appears, and for a while, it feels like a digital frontier — open, exciting, and even a little rebellious. You can reach the world for nothing. Then it grows. Millions join. Billions follow. And somewhere between the headlines and the IPO, the curtain drops, and the monetization begins.

It's a predictable cycle:
Free → Build a user base → Monetize with ads.

I've seen this pattern enough times that it barely surprises me anymore.

When **Facebook** first appeared, it was just a social network for college students. I remember signing up when it was still limited to Harvard and a few other universities. It felt small, almost innocent — a way to connect with classmates and share ideas. Mark Zuckerberg was still young, still experimenting, and none of us imagined that one day it would become a multibillion-dollar advertising machine capable of swaying global elections. But that's exactly what happened. Once the user base hit critical mass, free connectivity turned into the world's largest ad platform.

Then came **YouTube** — a place where ordinary people could upload silly videos or teach something useful. At first, it was a digital Wild West with no structure, no ads, and no gatekeepers. When Google bought it in 2006, the transformation began. Slowly, ads crept in. Today, YouTube generates over **$30 billion a year in ad revenue**, and every major brand on Earth budgets for it.

TikTok followed the same script. It began as a fun short-form video app where teenagers danced in their bedrooms. Then, as users exploded into the hundreds of millions, the platform introduced advertising, sponsorships, and influencer marketing. In 2025, analysts project TikTok will surpass **$32 billion in global ad revenue.** That's a staggering number for a company that didn't even exist fifteen years ago.

The pattern extends beyond social media. **Google Search** was once a clean white page with ten blue links — no clutter, no distractions. It became the backbone of the internet and now earns well over **$200 billion annually** from search advertising alone. What began as a free gateway to knowledge became one of the most profitable machines in history.

Every time, it's the same story. Start free. Build a massive audience. Then sell access to that audience.

The Platform Monetization Path

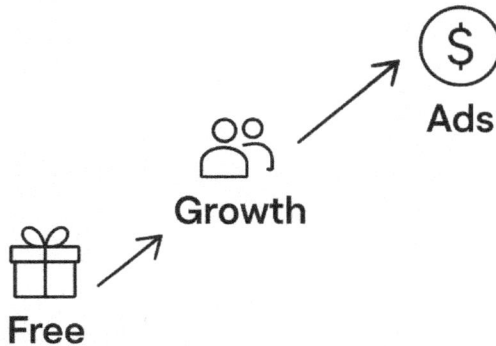

Every platform begins free, grows fast, and then monetizes attention.

That's not a criticism — it's a business reality. When you offer free access at global scale, the product eventually becomes **attention**. Someone will always pay to stand where everyone's looking.

And now we're seeing the next phase of this cycle play out with **artificial intelligence.**

Although you can pay for "Pro" versions, AI chatbots like **ChatGPT**, **Gemini**, **Claude**, and **Perplexity** are all in their "free and friendly" phase. They're building trust and user bases — hundreds of millions of conversations per day — but most are still operating at a loss. OpenAI, for example, reportedly spends **millions of dollars a day** to run its servers. That's not sustainable forever. Just like Facebook and Google before it, AI platforms will eventually turn to advertising, partnerships, and paid visibility. In fact, **Perplexity has already announced plans to include ads** once it reaches scale.

It's the same movie, just with smarter actors.

And that's why I bring this up early in the book. Because before the advertising floodgates open, there's a rare window of opportunity — right now — when AI results are still based primarily on **merit and meaning**, not money.

At this stage, what matters most is **being mentioned in the answers.**

That's your foothold into the future. If AI systems already understand your business, your content, and your authority *before* the ad era begins, you'll be ahead of 99 percent of competitors when monetization arrives. Because make no mistake — it will arrive.

So when you hear people say, "AI is free," just smile. We've seen this movie before:

Facebook was free.

YouTube was free.

TikTok was free.

Google Search was free.

Until it wasn't.

Every platform that wins our attention eventually charges for it. AI will be no different.

Key Takeaways:

If you don't pay for the product — you are the product.

Every major digital platform follows the same path: Free → Growth → Ads.

Advertising is not evil — it's the natural end state of success.

AI platforms are still in the "growth" phase, but the transition to paid advertisements is inevitable.

Until then, being mentioned organically in AI answers is the most valuable position a business can hold.

When the ads arrive — and they will — the brands already present in the conversation will have the ultimate advantage: they'll be trusted before they're sold.

Core Definitions & Terms

Words Matter

In every profession, from medicine to marketing, the vocabulary shapes how people think, act, and make decisions. Clear language leads to clear execution. Confusion leads to mistakes.

In the world of **Special Operations**, the right word can literally save lives. If a commander gives the wrong grid coordinate or a team leader misuses a term in a radio call, the consequences can be catastrophic. Every word carries weight.

I don't want to be overly dramatic about AI SEO — no one's life is on the line here — but **precision in language still matters**. We can't have an intelligent conversation about getting your business found by AI so you can get more customers and make more money unless we're speaking the same language.

Before we dive deeper, let's define the core vocabulary of this new era of search. These aren't buzzwords. They're the *operational terminology* that will help you see how AI search actually works — and how to make it work for you.

SEO (Search Engine Optimization)

Traditional SEO is the practice of making your web pages **easy for search engines to discover, understand, and rank**. It focuses on optimizing technical structure (titles, headers, metadata), content quality, and external signals like backlinks and reviews.

In the Google era, SEO success meant **ranking** — appearing high in a list of search results so humans would click through to your site.

AI SEO (Artificial Intelligence Search Engine Optimization)

AI SEO pursues the same goal—visibility—but the rules have changed. You're no longer fighting for clicks on a search results page; you're fighting for inclusion in AI-generated answers.

AI SEO is about preparing your content so that artificial intelligence systems (like ChatGPT, Gemini, or Perplexity) can **understand what you mean**, **trust what you say**, and **use your information** when composing their answers.

Think *inclusion and citation* — not ranking. The goal is to be the expert voice that the AI confidently quotes.

AEO / GEO / LLM SEO / AIDO

Different names for the same revolution:

AEO (Answer Engine Optimization): Focused on optimizing for AI systems that generate direct answers instead of showing a list of links.

GEO (Generative Engine Optimization): Centers on content crafted for generative models — AI that *creates* new text rather than merely retrieving existing pages.

LLM SEO: A technical term describing the process of optimizing content for **Large Language Models (LLMs)** specifically — the same AI engines that power tools like ChatGPT, Gemini, and Claude.

AIDO (AI Discovery Optimization): A newer, broader term that captures the full scope of visibility in the AI era —

27

ensuring your brand, data, and expertise are *discoverable* across all AI systems, not just answer engines. It's about being present wherever AI goes looking for trusted sources.

The practical differences between these terms are subtle, but the goal is the same: to help AI understand, trust, and surface your content. The industry hasn't settled on a single label yet — but the mission is universal.

LLM (Large Language Model)

An LLM is the brain behind most modern AI systems. It's trained on massive amounts of text to **predict the next most likely word** in a sentence — that's how it writes, reasons, and answers questions.

When you ask ChatGPT or Perplexity something, the LLM doesn't look up one answer; it generates a new one based on patterns, probability, and meaning learned from billions of examples.

Embedding

An embedding is how the AI **turns meaning into math**. Each word, sentence, image, or sound is converted into a **vector** — a long string of numbers representing its meaning. Two sentences with similar meaning will have similar numbers. This allows AI to compare concepts even if the exact words differ.

Embeddings are why an AI understands that "attorney" and "lawyer" are related, or that "near me" implies a local search.

Vector Database

A vector database is where those mathematical meanings live. Instead of storing text alphabetically or by keyword, it stores embeddings. When an AI system needs to answer a question, it queries the vector database to find the content that is *most similar in meaning* — not just the content that matches a keyword.

It's the foundation for how AI connects ideas, sources, and entities across the web.

RAG (Retrieval-Augmented Generation)

RAG is the secret weapon behind many AI systems today. It's a two-step process:

Retrieve relevant documents or data from a source (like the web, Wikipedia, or your own files).

Generate a natural-language answer using that information. This approach keeps the AI current and grounded in factual sources, rather than relying solely on what it learned during training.

Schema Markup (Structured Data)

When you open a website, you see words, images, and links. But behind the scenes, hidden inside the website's code, there's another layer of information written **for machines** — not for people. That layer is called **Schema Markup**, also known as **Structured Data**.

Let's break that down.

Websites are built using a language called **HTML**, which stands for **HyperText Markup Language**.

HTML is what tells your browser *how* to display information — what's a headline, what's a paragraph, what's a link, what's bold or italic. It's the skeleton of every webpage.

Now, **Schema Markup** is additional information embedded *inside* that HTML.

It doesn't change what visitors see, but it helps **AI systems and search engines** understand what the page *means*.

The most common format for writing schema is called **JSON-LD**, which stands for **JavaScript Object Notation for Linked Data**.

That sounds intimidating, but it's just a structured way of labeling data so computers can easily read it.

JSON-LD looks like a short paragraph of code inside curly brackets { }, written in plain text, that tells the AI, "This page describes a business named John's Mechanic Shop. It's a local service provider. Here's the address, phone number, opening hours, and reviews."

Let's look at an example.

What a human sees on the website:

John's Mechanic Shop
Family-owned auto repair in Springfield since 1985.
We specialize in oil changes, brake repair, and engine diagnostics.
Call (555) 123-4567 or visit us at 123 Main Street.

That's what *you* see when you visit the homepage.

But when an AI system — like Google, ChatGPT, or Perplexity — visits that same page, it doesn't "see" pretty fonts or colors.

It scans the code underneath the surface, reading a hidden layer of structured data like this:

```
<script type="application/ld+json">
{
 "@context": "https://schema.org",
 "@type": "AutoRepair",
 "name": "John's Mechanic Shop",
```

```
"image": "https://johnsmechanicshop.com/logo.jpg",
"address": {
"@type": "PostalAddress",
"streetAddress": "123 Main Street",
"addressLocality": "Springfield",
"addressRegion": "IL",
"postalCode": "62701"
},
"telephone": "+1-555-123-4567",
"openingHours": "Mo-Fr 08:00-17:00",
"priceRange": "$$"
}
</script>
```

That's Schema Markup in JSON-LD form.

It's invisible to human visitors but clear as daylight to machines.

When an AI or search crawler reads that snippet, it knows exactly who John is, what he does, where he operates, when he's open, and even what type of business category he belongs to ("AutoRepair").

Think of Schema Markup as **a translation guide between your business and the machines that describe it to the world.**

Without it, the AI might have to guess what your page means.

With it, there's no guessing. You're telling the system precisely what it needs to know.

If you want your business to be *understood* and *trusted* by AI systems, Schema is one of the most valuable tools you can implement — even if you never write a line of code yourself. Many website builders and SEO plugins (like Yoast or RankMath) include easy fields where you simply fill in your business details, and they automatically create the schema code for you behind the scenes.

FAQ Schema (Frequently Asked Questions)

Let's shift from "what your business is" to "what your customers ask."

Every industry has questions that come up again and again:

"How much does it cost to replace brake pads?"

"Do you offer same-day service?"

"Do you guarantee your work?"

These are called Frequently Asked Questions (FAQs).

When you post FAQs on your website, you're helping human visitors find quick answers — and you're also helping AI systems understand your expertise.

Just like Schema Markup describes *your business,* FAQ Schema describes *the questions and answers* you provide. It tells search engines, "This section is a list of common questions, each with a clear answer."

Here's how that looks.

What a human sees:

Frequently Asked Questions
Q: Do you offer same-day repairs?
A: Yes. In most cases, if you bring your car in before 10 a.m., we can complete repairs by the end of the day.

Q: What forms of payment do you accept?
A: We accept cash, credit cards, and digital payments like Apple Pay.

That's what your customers read on the page.

But here's what an AI system reads in the hidden schema layer:

```
<script type="application/ld+json">
{
 "@context": "https://schema.org",
 "@type": "FAQPage",
```

```
"mainEntity": [
{
"@type": "Question",
"name": "Do you offer same-day repairs?",
"acceptedAnswer": {
"@type": "Answer",
"text": "Yes. In most cases, if you bring your car in before 10 a.m., we
can complete repairs by the end of the day."
}
},
{
"@type": "Question",
"name": "What forms of payment do you accept?",
"acceptedAnswer": {
"@type": "Answer",
"text": "We accept cash, credit cards, and digital payments like Apple
Pay."
}
}
]
}
</script>
```

That's FAQ Schema. It's the machine-readable version of your human-friendly Q & A section.

When you include FAQ Schema correctly, two things happen:

AI systems can extract and quote your answers directly in search results or AI-generated responses.

Your expertise becomes visible — not just to people, but to the algorithms shaping what information appears in front of them.

This is especially powerful because AI loves **questions and answers.** It's how people naturally communicate — and how AI systems naturally organize knowledge.

In the future, as AI-powered assistants become the default interface for local and global search, having clear, structured FAQ data will make the difference between being *mentioned in the answer* and being *invisible*.

Let's make a quick schema summary:

HTML shows *how* content appears to humans.

Schema Markup (in JSON-LD) explains *what* that content means to machines.

FAQ Schema labels your *questions and answers* so AI can read, understand, and cite them correctly.

Humans read what's on the page.

AI reads what's in the code.

Schema is the bridge between the two.

*** We will discuss Schema in greater detail in chapter: O — Optimization: Make Your Message Machine-Readable

---

Knowledge Graph

A **Knowledge Graph** is how AI systems organize the world's information.

It's a massive network of **entities** — people, places, organizations, and things — connected by relationships. Google, Microsoft, and OpenAI all maintain their own versions.

The more clearly your business is represented in that graph — through consistent names, locations, and links — the more "real" you appear to AI.

Entity

An entity is anything that can be uniquely identified. It could be your **business**, a **product**, a **service**, or even **you** as an author or expert.

Entities give AI an anchor point. When the system reads your content, it looks for signals that confirm you're an actual business with a physical location, a website, and a reputation.

Topic Cluster

A **topic cluster** is how you organize authority.

It's a structure where one central "hub" page covers a topic broadly (like *Home Security Systems*), and several shorter "spoke" pages dive into subtopics (*Wireless Alarms, Smart Locks, Security Cameras*).

Together, they show AI that you have depth of expertise and a clear internal logic — both critical for establishing trust.

Zero-Click

A **zero-click** result happens when the user gets their answer directly from a search or AI response — without ever visiting your website.

As AI-driven answers become the norm, zero-click interactions are increasing dramatically. Your visibility in these answers matters more than your traditional web traffic metrics.

AI Citation

An **AI citation** is when your content is referenced or quoted as a source in an AI-generated answer.

It's the new "Page 1 ranking." You might not get a click, but your name, brand, or URL appears in the answer that millions of users read.

Fan-Out Searches

When you ask an AI a question, it doesn't run a single search. It performs a **fan-out** — sending multiple queries across databases, APIs, and web sources to collect context before generating its answer.

For example, imagine someone on vacation with a sudden toothache. They type, *"Find a dentist near me who accepts cash for an emergency visit."* The AI won't rely on one data source. It may fan out to:

➢ Google Maps for nearby dental offices,

➢ Health or insurance databases for coverage options,

➢ Local business directories for reviews and hours,

➢ The practice's website for pricing or payment details, and

➢ Recent forum posts or articles about emergency dental care in that city.

Each run can generate a slightly different fan-out, which means results can shift from moment to moment. That's why optimizing for a single keyword is obsolete. You must build **strong, consistent context** across every topic, platform, and page to be included in the answers that matter.

Answer Reliability (Confidence)

AI systems evaluate how "confident" they are in their answers. That confidence is based on factors like source consistency, factual alignment, and clarity of writing.

Pages with verifiable claims, schema markup, and clean structure tend to score higher in this invisible metric — making them more likely to be quoted.

E-E-A-T (Experience, Expertise, Authority, Trust)

This framework originated with Google but now influences all AI systems.

Experience: Have you personally done what you're talking about?

Expertise: Do you demonstrate deep knowledge?

Authority: Do others cite or recognize you?

Trust: Are your claims consistent and verifiable?

E-E-A-T is how AI measures *credibility*, and it's one of the most important factors for being included in an answer.

Local Signals

Local signals are your **digital proof of existence.** They include your **Google Business Profile**, map listings, Yelp reviews, Chamber of Commerce entries, LinkedIn company page, and even your street address and phone number consistency across the web.

To AI, these details confirm that you're not just a website — you're a real business serving real people.

TL;DR

TL;DR stands for "Too Long; Didn't Read."

It's a short, high-impact summary that gives readers the essence of your article in 3–5 sentences (or a few bullet points).

A good TL;DR helps busy readers decide whether to keep reading or gives them the main takeaways immediately. It's also great for AI SEO because it signals to AI systems like

ChatGPT and Perplexity exactly what your article is about—increasing your chances of being summarized accurately or featured in AI search results.

You can call this section the **TL;DR** if you have a tech audience, an **"Executive Summary"** if you have a professional audience, or **"What You'll Learn in This Article"** to be SEO and user friendly. Either way, be clear about what the article is about, who it is for, and the key takeaways.

Example: an article from a Real Estate Blogger in Arizona.

Buying a home near a golf course offers scenic views and higher property values—but also unique challenges like HOA fees, errant golf balls, and privacy concerns. This article walks you through what to consider before purchasing, including resale potential, noise levels, and insurance coverage. Learn how to find the perfect balance between lifestyle and long-term investment.

Key Takeaways:

Words define clarity; clarity defines credibility.

You can't influence a system you don't understand. Mastering this vocabulary gives you a shared language with the machines that now mediate attention and trust.

How AI Search Works

Remember when I told you that I love **reverse-engineering** things — figuring out how systems actually work so you can make them work better for you? That mindset is exactly what we're doing here.

We just went over the definitions and key terms, and yes, you'll see some of them again in this chapter. That's intentional. The goal now isn't to define them — it's to show how they interact, overlap, and drive the AI search ecosystem as a whole.

My purpose isn't to turn you into an AI scientist or software engineer. It's to help you see the system clearly enough to use it strategically — to understand what's happening behind the curtain so you can position your business in a way that AI recognizes, trusts, and includes in its answers.

Because once you understand the system, you stop guessing — and you start **engineering outcomes**.

At a high level, AI search engines don't retrieve information the way Google used to.

They don't look for exact keyword matches. They **predict** — using patterns, probabilities, and meaning.

When you type a question like "What's the best Italian restaurant near me?" traditional Google might look for pages that include those exact words: *"best," "Italian," "restaurant," "near," "me."*

It scans millions of pages, scores them, and ranks them by relevance.

But AI search — whether it's ChatGPT, Gemini, or Perplexity — does something far more complex and intelligent. It tries to **understand what you mean**, not just what you said.

It looks at your words and turns them into *data about meaning.*

From Words to Meaning: Embeddings

Here's how that translation works.

Every sentence you write, every word on your website, even every image you post, can be represented as a **mathematical vector** — a long string of numbers that encode its *meaning*. This process is called **embedding.**

If you've ever used a map app on your phone, think of embeddings as the GPS coordinates of language.

Each piece of content — a word, phrase, or image — is given a unique location in "meaning space." Two points that are close together represent ideas that mean roughly the same thing. "Mechanic" and "auto repair shop" might sit next to each other. "Attorney" and "lawyer" overlap. "Good," "great," and "excellent" all live in the same neighborhood.

That's how AI understands language contextually. It doesn't care about spelling or capitalization — it cares about **semantic distance**: how close your content is to the *idea* someone is asking about.

The Role of Vector Databases

Once the AI has converted everything into embeddings, it stores them inside something called a **vector database** — a specialized system designed to **compare meaning** instead of text.

When a user asks a question, the AI doesn't simply look up keywords.

It searches the vector database for *nearby meanings*.

It asks, "What other pieces of text live close to this concept?"

So if someone asks, "Who's the most reliable plumber in Austin?" the system doesn't need your website to literally say "most reliable plumber in Austin."

It can understand that your page about *"licensed plumbing services with 24-hour response times in Austin"* is semantically related — and may actually be a better match.

That's why your writing style matters. The clearer, more conversational, and more natural your explanations are, the easier it is for AI systems to correctly map your meaning and include you in their results.

Retrieval-Augmented Generation (RAG): How AI Stays Updated

Now let's add another layer: **RAG**, which stands for **Retrieval-Augmented Generation.**

When you ask a modern AI assistant a question, it doesn't rely solely on what it already knows.

Instead, it performs a **two-step process**:

Retrieval – It quickly searches trusted sources or live databases to collect relevant facts, articles, or documents (sometimes even from your website if it's accessible).

Generation – It then uses that retrieved information to **compose a new, natural-language answer** tailored to your question.

This allows AI systems to stay somewhat current — referencing the most relevant, high-confidence information available — while still using their trained intelligence to write coherent answers.

Think of it like briefing a commander: first, you gather intelligence from multiple sources; then, you synthesize it into a concise, actionable report. That's RAG — intelligence gathering followed by analysis and presentation.

For business owners, this means **your content can directly influence the generation stage** if it's structured clearly enough to be retrieved in the first step.

Conversational Context and Clarity

Because AI search is meaning-based, **context and clarity are everything.**

The AI reads your pages almost like a human — scanning for cues about *who you are, what you do, where you operate, and why someone should trust you.*

Pages that plainly explain these things are easier for AI systems to interpret correctly.

You might have heard me say before that "clarity is the new keyword."

That's not a slogan — it's a truth about how machine comprehension works.

AI systems don't respond to trickery, keyword stuffing, or hidden text. They respond to structure, simplicity, and truth that's verifiable across multiple sources.

Mentions and citations — on your own site, in directories, on LinkedIn, in reviews, or in local media — all feed into how confident the AI becomes that your business is legitimate. In the old world, **backlinks** were the currency of authority. In the new world, **citations** and **consistent identity signals** are the proof of trustworthiness.

These signals feed into the knowledge graphs that shape AI understanding.

When multiple credible sources describe you the same way, you form a distinct, verifiable "entity" inside the **knowledge graph** — the massive web of relationships AI uses to understand the world.

Once you exist there, you're not just a business — you're part of the machine's understanding of reality.

Fan-Out Searches and Variability

Here's another fascinating part: when you ask an AI assistant a question, it rarely runs a single search.

It performs what's called a **fan-out** — dozens of micro-searches and background checks that expand outward across multiple sources, APIs, and databases.

One query might check Wikipedia. Another might query Yelp. Another might reference Google Maps. Another might access a vector database.

It then pulls together all these micro-results, weighs them for reliability, and merges them into a unified answer.

That's why if you ask the same AI the same question twice, you might get slightly different responses.

Each fan-out can touch a different mix of data sources, and since AI is probabilistic (based on likelihood rather than certainty), no two runs are identical.

This variation isn't an error — it's a feature.

It's the machine exploring the space of meaning, the way a human might read three different news stories before deciding what's true.

What All This Means for You

If you take away nothing else from this chapter, remember this: **AI doesn't count your words — it interprets your meaning.**

That's the new frontier of visibility.

It's not about whether your headline has the perfect keyword density or your meta tag matches your competitors'. It's about whether your entire body of content consistently tells a clear, trustworthy, verifiable story about who you are and what you do.

In the same way that a good commander learns to brief with clarity and confidence — not volume — a good business learns to speak to AI systems with structure and authenticity.

The clearer you communicate your expertise, the more likely it is that AI search engines will cite, reference, and recommend you when customers go looking for solutions.

Key Takeaways:

*AI search engines **predict meaning**, not match keywords.*

*They turn language into **embeddings** and use **vector databases** to find related ideas.*

***RAG** allows them to retrieve current data before composing an answer.*

***Clarity, consistency, and context** are stronger than keyword repetition.*

***Fan-out searches** mean results vary — optimizing for one phrase is obsolete.*

The new measure of success is whether AI systems understand you, not whether they rank you.

*In short: **AI is learning what you mean — not tallying which words you typed.***

Top AI Models and Platforms

I still remember the first essay I ever wrote on a computer — not a typewriter.

I was a university student writing an English Literature paper on Shakespeare's *Henry V* – the clunky desktop computer had a greenish monitor and a keyboard that sounded like a typewriter.

At the time, it felt revolutionary. I could edit paragraphs without retyping the entire page. I thought technology couldn't get much better than that.

A year or two later, I got my first **AOL** account. It came with that iconic dial-up sound — a digital screech that meant I was connecting to the world. AOL felt unstoppable. It was the largest email provider on earth. Everyone I knew had an "@aol.com" address. We thought it would last forever.

Then came **MySpace**, which let us create personal websites, add music, and connect with friends. It felt like a digital party. But today, barely anyone remembers it. The same thing happened to AOL — once dominant, now largely forgotten.

Technology evolves fast — sometimes faster than we can emotionally adjust.

We moved from a blue screen with white letters to high-definition websites with images, videos, and AI chatbots that talk back. What was "the future" five years ago becomes yesterday's news in a heartbeat.

That's why, as I write this book, I want to emphasize a truth that will still hold years from now: **The platforms we talk about today might not be the same ones we talk about tomorrow.**

But understanding the top AI models right now will help you see *how* they work, *who* runs them, and *why* they matter for your business.

Some of these systems are built by trillion-dollar enterprises. Others are niche, purpose-built, or open-source collaborations.

All of them share one thing: they're competing to become the gateway to the world's knowledge.

So let's look at the **current top AI platforms and models**, knowing full well that this landscape will keep shifting — just as it did from AOL to MySpace to Facebook to TikTok.

OpenAI — ChatGPT and the GPT-4 / GPT-5 Family

Founded: 2015, backed by Microsoft and other major investors.

Approach: Make artificial intelligence accessible, conversational, and useful for everyday people.

Flagship Models: GPT-4, GPT-4 Turbo, and the evolving GPT-5.

Core Features: Text, image, code, and now real-time voice capabilities.

Strengths: Exceptional at reasoning, creativity, summarization, and dialogue.

Business Impact: Deep integration across Microsoft products — Word, Excel, Outlook, and Bing Copilot.

ChatGPT introduced the world to the idea of *talking to the internet*. For small businesses, it became the easiest on-ramp into AI SEO — because every time someone asks, "What's the best local gym in Tampa?" the model decides whose content gets mentioned.

Google — Gemini (formerly Bard)

Founded: 2023 (as Bard), rebranded to Gemini in 2024.

Parent Company: Alphabet.

Approach: Build AI directly into the world's information infrastructure.

Model Family: Gemini 1.5 Pro, Flash, and Nano — tuned for reasoning, speed, and mobile performance.

Strengths: Unmatched integration with Search, Maps, YouTube, Gmail, and Android.

Business Impact: Gemini's AI Overviews appear at the top of Google Search — making visibility inside Gemini effectively the new SEO.

If ChatGPT is the assistant, Gemini is the infrastructure — the quiet engine deciding what billions of people see first.

Anthropic — The Claude Family

Founded: 2021 by former OpenAI engineers.

Approach: "Constitutional AI" — models designed to reason ethically and safely.

Models: Claude 1 → 2 → 3, with multimodal (text, code, image) capabilities.

Strengths: Analytical reasoning, comprehension, and tone; trusted by legal, research, and consulting fields.

Business Impact: Claude powers numerous enterprise tools that let teams query internal data in plain language — a major advantage for knowledge-driven businesses.

Where ChatGPT is imaginative, Claude is disciplined. It's the AI that reads every word before it answers.

Microsoft Copilot (Powered by OpenAI)

Founded: Microsoft, in partnership with OpenAI.

Approach: Integrate AI directly into the workplace.

Core Features: Embedded in Microsoft 365, Windows 11, Bing, and Edge. Drafts emails, summarizes documents, analyzes spreadsheets, and builds presentations.

Strengths: Seamless productivity — AI where work already happens.

Business Impact: For business owners, Copilot removes the barrier between "doing work" and "using AI." It's built-in, invisible, and transformative.

Because Copilot uses GPT-4 Turbo, it's not just an assistant — it's a search engine with context. If Bing Copilot recommends your company in response to a query, that's AI SEO in motion.

Perplexity.ai — Built on Trust and Citation

Founded: 2022 by engineers from OpenAI, DeepMind, and Meta.

Approach: Combine conversational AI with transparent sourcing.

Core Features: Real-time internet retrieval and citation beneath every response.

Strengths: Academic-grade accuracy and transparency.

Business Impact: If your content is structured clearly with schema markup and expertise signals, Perplexity may cite you directly — the equivalent of being footnoted by the future.

Perplexity is the antidote to blind trust. It shows its homework — and rewards those who write clearly enough to be cited.

Meta — LLaMA and the Meta AI Ecosystem

Founded: Meta Platforms (formerly Facebook).

Approach: Democratize AI through open-source models and social integration.

Model Family: LLaMA 1 → 3 (Large Language Model Meta AI).

Core Features: Multimodal reasoning, text and image generation, open-weight availability for developers.

Strengths: Openness and global reach — billions of daily users across Facebook, Instagram, and WhatsApp.

Business Impact: Meta's scale means that every post, tag, and interaction helps train its algorithms to recognize real-world entities — including your brand.

Meta is turning social engagement into structured intelligence. Every like, share, and reply strengthens its understanding of what people value.

Meta AI Integration in WhatsApp (Global Launch 2025)

Founded: WhatsApp (2009); acquired by Meta in 2014.

Approach: Bring conversational AI to billions through the app people already use daily.

Core Features:
• AI assistant embedded directly in chat threads.
• Real-time translation, summarization, and Q & A.
• Contextual recommendations for local products and services.
• WhatsApp Business tools for automated responses, scheduling, and support.

Strengths: Frictionless, natural, and omnipresent — AI that lives where communication already happens.

Business Impact: Every business conversation inside WhatsApp is now a training signal for Meta's discovery algorithms.

Your chat tone, product descriptions, and response time all shape how Meta understands and recommends you.

In short: your customer service inbox is now part of your AI SEO strategy.

Mistral — The European Challenger

Founded: 2023, Paris, France.

Approach: Build open-weight models that companies can host privately — ensuring data sovereignty and compliance with EU law.

Notable Model: Mixtral 8×7B — a "mixture-of-experts" system that balances speed and efficiency.

Strengths: Lightweight, fast, and open; ideal for startups, governments, and research labs.

Business Impact: Mistral symbolizes Europe's response to U.S. AI dominance — transparent, ethical, and locally controlled. Expect more regional players to follow this path.

DeepSeek, Databricks DBRX, and the Open Model Movement

Founded: DeepSeek (China), Databricks DBRX (U.S.), with global contributors.

Approach: Keep AI open and affordable.

Core Models: DeepSeek for cost-efficient reasoning; DBRX for enterprise-grade analytics.

Strengths: Customizable, privacy-friendly, and scalable.

Business Impact: These models ensure that small and medium-sized businesses aren't locked out of the AI race. They can deploy private models tailored to their data — no Silicon Valley dependency required.

Open models prevent monopoly. They keep innovation honest.

Apple — Apple Intelligence (iOS 18, June 2025)

Founded: 1976.

Approach: Private, on-device AI that prioritizes user control and seamless integration.

Core Features:
• Integrated across iOS 18, macOS, and iPadOS.
• Combines Siri with generative rewriting, summarization, and context awareness.
• Performs local tasks on-device; uses secure cloud LLMs for complex reasoning.
• Optional integration with OpenAI's ChatGPT for advanced dialogue.

Strengths: Privacy-first design that quietly enhances productivity without harvesting data.

Business Impact: Apple Intelligence changes discovery. When users ask Siri, "Find the best coffee shop near me," Apple's ecosystem may answer without touching Google.

For business owners, optimizing Apple Maps listings, app data, and verified contact info is now essential to AI visibility.

Amazon — Alexa and the Generative Commerce Revolution

Founded: 1994.

Approach: Voice-first commerce powered by contextual AI.

Core Features:
• Generative recommendations across shopping, media, and smart-home devices.
• Summarizes reviews, compares products, and interprets intent.
• Deep integration with Amazon Business and Seller Central.

Strengths: Commercial fluency — Alexa bridges search, suggestion, and purchase in one conversation.

Business Impact: Visibility in Amazon's generative system depends on clarity and credibility.

Well-written product listings, strong reviews, and structured metadata all raise your chances of being the product Alexa recommends next.

The Big Picture

Each of these models has its own strengths:

OpenAI dominates creativity and reasoning.

Google Gemini dominates infrastructure and search visibility.

Anthropic Claude dominates safety and comprehension.

Perplexity dominates citation and trust.

Meta LLaMA dominates openness and social scale.

Mistral & DeepSeek lead the innovation frontier.

Microsoft Copilot leads integration into daily work.

Apple Intelligence defines privacy-driven design.

Amazon Alexa drives commercial discovery.

Together, they form the living ecosystem rewriting how knowledge is created, interpreted, and shared.

Like AOL and MySpace before them, some will fade. Others will dominate for decades. But the lesson is constant:

Platforms change. Principles don't.

Clarity, authority, and trust remain timeless.

Whether the answers come from ChatGPT, Gemini, or something we haven't heard of yet, those same traits will decide whose voices are found — and whose disappear.

Key Takeaways

AI platforms evolve as fast as past technologies — what dominates today may vanish tomorrow.

Knowing the top players helps you understand where and how your business can be discovered.

Some AIs (like Perplexity) cite their sources; others (like Gemini) are the search.

The companies shaping AI are, in effect, shaping discovery itself.

Just as AOL gave way to Gmail and MySpace to Instagram, the leaders of 2026 may not survive 2030.

Stay curious. Stay adaptable. You don't have to predict the future — just be ready for it.

What's Changing (or Not) in SEO

Ten years ago, almost every car on the road ran on gasoline. You filled the tank, you changed the oil, and you didn't think twice about it. Then something happened — **Tesla.**

Before long, the Toyota Prius made "hybrid" a household word, and soon every major automaker was promising an electric line. Fast-forward to today: you can still buy a car with four doors, five seat belts, and four wheels — it'll still get you from point A to point B — but *how* it gets there has completely changed.

The engine is different. The maintenance is different. Even the business model — charging stations, government incentives, software updates — is different.

That's exactly what's happening to SEO right now.

Search still gets people from "question" to "answer," from "problem" to "solution." But under the hood, the engine that powers discovery has changed. Traditional SEO isn't dead — it's just being re-engineered.

Let's look under that hood.

Disruption Is Certain

There's no gentle way to say it: the entire landscape of online visibility is being rewritten.

For 25 years, Google has been the gatekeeper of digital attention. But with the rise of AI search, users no longer need to *browse* to find what they want — they just *ask*.

In early 2024, AI-generated summaries began appearing directly in Google results as "AI Overviews." By 2025, they're becoming the default for many queries. Platforms like **ChatGPT**, **Perplexity**, and **Gemini** are accelerating this shift by giving users complete answers — not lists of links.

That means the "click economy" that powered digital marketing for decades is declining. Instead of ten blue links, there's often *one* synthesized answer. And inside that answer, maybe only two or three brands are mentioned.

That's disruption. Not theoretical — actual.

Evolution of Search

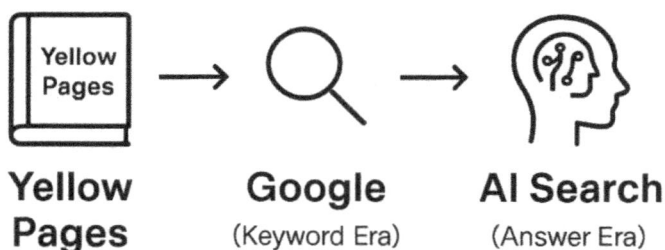

Yellow Pages   **Google** (Keyword Era)   **AI Search** (Answer Era)

From Keywords to Conversations

Traditional SEO revolved around keywords — specific phrases people typed into Google. "Best pizza in Chicago." "How to fix a leaky faucet." "Cheap flights to Rome."

But AI doesn't think in keywords. It thinks in **meaning** and **context.**

Instead of counting how many times you use a phrase, AI models interpret *what you're trying to say.*

They map your words into relationships — who, what, where, why — and try to answer the *intent* behind the question, not the exact wording.

That's why **conversational language** now matters more than keyword density.

If your website sounds robotic, stuffed with repetitive keywords, AI systems won't understand it as well as a natural, human explanation.

Writing for AI means writing *for clarity,* not for algorithms.

Competing for Answers Instead of Clicks

In the old SEO game, you wanted to rank #1 on Google. The logic was simple: more clicks = more traffic = more sales.

In the AI world, **ranking doesn't exist** in the same way. You're not fighting for a position on a list; you're fighting for **inclusion** in an answer.

When an AI assistant generates a response — "What's the best security system for small businesses?" — it doesn't show 10 links. It composes a 2 – 3 paragraph summary and, if you're lucky, cites the source.

That means your goal isn't to "rank higher." It's to **be referenced.**

You want the AI to say, **"According to BeFoundByAISearch.com..."** or **"Based on insights from the AI SEO strategist at BeFoundByAISearch.com..."**

That's the new form of digital authority — being *quoted* by the machine instead of just *ranked* by the algorithm.

Those mentions, or **AI citations**, are the new form of digital authority.

AI Is Driving Both Traffic and Sales

AI search isn't just influencing discovery — it's starting to **control consumer decisions.**

When people use AI assistants to plan trips, buy products, or compare services, those systems can make personalized recommendations instantly. Instead of clicking through five pages of results, the user gets a confident, trustworthy suggestion — sometimes with affiliate links already embedded.

By 2026, analysts predict that **over half of online purchases will be influenced or initiated by AI-generated recommendations.** (Statista, 2025 projection).

That's why appearing in AI-driven answers isn't just a matter of visibility — it's a matter of *revenue*. If you're not visible in those ecosystems, you won't just lose traffic — you'll lose sales.

Focus on Hundreds of Questions, Not One Keyword

In traditional SEO, businesses obsessed over one keyword at a time. "Plumber Denver." "Dentist Austin." "Yoga classes Miami."

But AI doesn't operate at the keyword level — it operates at the **topic level.**

It doesn't care if you said "plumber" or "pipe repair." It cares whether you *cover the topic comprehensively*.

The winning strategy now is to build **topic clusters** — groups of interconnected pages that explain every angle of your expertise.

For example:

A home security company might create a hub page on "Home Security Systems" and smaller articles on "DIY vs Professional Installation," "Best Smart Locks for 2026," "Cybersecurity for Small Businesses," and "Physical Security Checklists."

Together, those pieces signal depth, authority, and relevance.

That's what AI looks for: **breadth plus depth.**

From Ten Hyperlinks to One Answer

We used to compete for "Page One."

Now we're competing for the **paragraph** inside the answer.

Search engines are no longer pages of choices — they're conversations.

When someone asks a question, the AI gives one best answer, maybe two secondary citations.

That's why you need to think in terms of *being quoted*, not *being clicked.*

Your reward isn't the hyperlink — it's the **mention** that shapes public perception.

And if that feels unfamiliar, remember this: the rules always change, but the mission never does — communicate clearly, serve your audience, and be trustworthy enough that both humans and machines want to quote you.

What's Staying the Same in SEO

If you've read this far, you might be thinking, "Well, everything's changing — so does traditional SEO even matter anymore?"

Yes, it absolutely does.

Just as electric cars still have wheels, doors, and seat belts, **the fundamentals of SEO still apply.**

You still need structure. You still need trust. You still need relevance.

AI might be driving the vehicle now, but it's driving on the same roads.

"If You Aren't Paying for the Product — You Are the Product."

This saying has been true since the dawn of the internet. Every free platform — from Facebook to TikTok to AI chatbots — eventually monetizes *you.*

AI companies are already preparing to do the same. Perplexity has announced future ads; OpenAI is building partnerships with major brands.

Free access builds user data. User data builds value. Value drives advertising.

That cycle hasn't changed in 25 years — only the interface has.

The Advertising Cycle Remains the Same

Just as we discussed in *The Progress of Advertising,* the free-to-paid transition always follows the same arc:

Launch for free → Grow user base → Introduce ads → Optimize for engagement.

Google, YouTube, Facebook, Instagram, and TikTok all followed this pattern.

AI platforms are next in line.

When that happens, being cited organically — *before* the ads appear — will be your single greatest competitive advantage.

70% of AI Results Still Reference Top 10 Traditional SEO Sources

Despite the hype, the backbone of AI-generated content still comes from **traditional web pages.**

A recent Search Engine Journal study found that roughly **70% of AI-generated answers cite the same domains** that dominate Google's first page.

In other words, **SEO authority still feeds AI visibility.**

The best-structured, highest-credibility pages are still the data sources AI trusts the most.

If your site already ranks well in traditional search, you have a head start in AI SEO.

Traditional SEO Still Matters — AI SEO Is an Additional Layer

Think of AI SEO as the *next gear* in the same transmission.

You still need:

Fast-loading, mobile-friendly pages.

Clear headlines and well-organized content.

Schema markup and meta descriptions.

Credible backlinks and local business listings.

Those remain the foundation.

AI SEO adds a new layer — **semantic clarity, conversational tone, and structured context** — but it builds on the same chassis.

So don't abandon SEO; **upgrade it.** The difference between the businesses that thrive in the next five years and the ones that fade will be this — who adapts fastest without forgetting the fundamentals.

Will AI Make Google Obsolete?

No — not even close.

If there's one thing history has shown us, it's that **Google always adapts.** This is a billion-dollar company built on turning human curiosity into a monetizable product, and they've mastered that art better than anyone.

Google didn't just create a search engine — it created an entire **economic ecosystem of visibility.** They figured out how to transform every search, every click, and every moment of attention into measurable, billable data. From AdWords to YouTube ads, Google turned information into currency.

When people say, *"AI is going to kill Google,"* I smile. Because that's exactly what people said when social media arrived, when voice assistants took off, and when apps started replacing browsers. Yet here we are — and Google is still the front door of the internet.

Will AI reduce some of Google's traditional ad revenue? Absolutely.

Businesses that used to pay for top-page placements or cost-per-click campaigns may see fewer impressions as AI assistants deliver direct answers instead of lists.

But here's the truth: **Google will find new ways to monetize AI search.**

They've already started. Those "AI Overviews" you see in your search results? That's not a beta test — that's Google preparing the next evolution of its business model. They're going to integrate ads, sponsored AI recommendations, and premium data sources into those results. In other words, they're not losing the game — they're rewriting it.

And remember: Google owns more **data** about human behavior than any company in history.

Every **Android phone** reports anonymized usage and location patterns.

Every **Google search** teaches the algorithm more about what people want.

Every **YouTube video** watched reveals preferences, habits, and interests.

Every **Google Maps query** tells them where people actually go, not just what they say they like.

That depth of data makes Google's AI models exceptionally powerful — and incredibly difficult to compete with.

While new players like **Perplexity** or **Anthropic's Claude** may innovate on speed or transparency, Google's advantage is **scale and integration.** Their systems are everywhere — in your browser, your phone, your car, and your smart home devices.

So no, AI won't make Google obsolete. It will make Google even more intelligent — and even more profitable.

The challenge for business owners is not to fight Google's evolution; it's to **work with it.**

That means ensuring your business — your products, services, and expertise — are fully optimized so that Google's AI systems can find, understand, and include you in the answers it generates.

That's the mission of **FoundByAISearch.com** — helping you understand how to be *visible* in this new landscape. Because the rules are changing, but the goal remains the same: **be found, get clients, and make more money.**

Key Takeaway:

AI hasn't ended SEO; it's evolving it.

We've moved from chasing clicks to earning inclusion — from ranking for phrases to being trusted for knowledge.

The tactics have changed. The purpose hasn't.

SEO's **core principles** *— clarity, credibility, and structure — are timeless.*

AI SEO is not a replacement; it's an evolutionary layer.

The advertising cycle, trust signals, and ranking authority remain relevant.

Traditional SEO still feeds the AI systems that generate answers.

In short: **SEO didn't die. It evolved.**

The smart move isn't to start over — it's to keep building, one structured signal at a time, until the algorithms and the audience both know who you are.

Google isn't going away — it's evolving. Expect a blended world of **traditional search + AI answers**, *powered by smarter algorithms and new ad models. The key to success isn't predicting the next disruption — it's positioning yourself so that, no matter what Google becomes, it can still find you.*

The FOUND Framework

Wow — that was a lot of background information.

If you've made it this far, you've already covered more about AI search than most digital marketers ever will. And if some of it felt dense or new, that's perfectly fine. You're not supposed to memorize every acronym or remember every model name.

Like anything worth mastering, understanding AI SEO takes a little repetition. You might find yourself coming back to certain sections — rereading them once, maybe twice — and each time, something new will click. The more you study how these systems think, the faster you'll start to *see* the patterns. Before long, you'll recognize how to work with AI instead of against it.

So now that we've covered the theory — the what, why, and how — it's time to move into the **practical side** of this book: how to make sure *you* are found by AI ... so you can get more clients and make more money.

This next section introduces a simple five-step process I call the **FOUND Framework.**

FOUND Framework

F - **Foundation:** Build an Unshakable Digital Presence

O - **Optimization:** Make Your Message Machine-Readable

U - **Utility:** Create Content That Solves Human Problems

N - **Niche Authority:** Establish Unquestionable Expertise

D - **Data-Driven Improvements:** Measure, Adapt, Scale

It's the foundation for everything that follows — a roadmap to help your business build visibility, trust, and authority in the age of AI-driven discovery.

Each letter represents a core principle you can apply immediately:

F — Foundation: Build an Unshakable Digital Presence

Everything begins with structure. Your foundation is the framework that determines whether AI systems can find, crawl, and interpret your presence online. It includes clear navigation, consistent branding, fast loading speeds, mobile responsiveness, secure hosting (HTTPS), and properly configured metadata.

Think of it as the architecture of your digital command post — the systems, logistics, and layout that everything else depends on. If your site is disorganized, slow, or unstable, AI won't trust it. A strong foundation ensures your business is discoverable, dependable, and ready to grow.

O — Optimization: Make Your Message Machine-Readable

Once the foundation is solid, optimization fine-tunes how your site communicates with machines. This is where you translate meaning into code. AI search engines rely on structured signals — things like **schema markup**, **semantic organization**, **internal linking**, and **entity relationships** — to understand who you are, what you offer, and why it matters.

Optimization turns content into data. It aligns your words, structure, and context so that both humans and machines interpret them the same way. When your message is properly optimized, AI doesn't have to guess — it knows exactly where you fit, and it can confidently include you in the answers it provides.

U — Utility: Create Content That Solves Human Problems

Usefulness is the new currency of visibility. AI systems are trained to prioritize content that genuinely helps people. This means writing with the reader in mind — anticipating their questions; offering practical guidance; and sharing your real-world experience.

When you serve your audience well, AI learns to trust you as a reliable source of answers.

N — Niche Authority: Establish Unquestionable Expertise

The internet rewards general knowledge, but **AI rewards specialized expertise.**

This step is about building *topic clusters* and *entity signals* that define your authority within a niche. Whether you're a plumber, a real estate agent, or a cybersecurity consultant, the goal is to become unmistakably known for something.

Niche authority tells AI: *"This person doesn't just talk about this subject — they own it."*

D — Data-Driven Improvements: Measure, Adapt, Scale

Finally, nothing in AI SEO is static.

Algorithms evolve, user behavior shifts, and competitors adapt. That's why the last step — **Data-Driven**

Improvements — focuses on tracking performance and refining your strategy.

You'll learn to interpret analytics, measure engagement, identify which pages are being cited or mentioned by AI systems, and use that data to continuously improve your visibility.

This is how you stay ahead of the curve — by letting the numbers guide your next move.

The **FOUND Framework** is designed to be simple, actionable, and repeatable. You don't need to be a coder or a marketing expert to apply it. You just need curiosity, discipline, and the willingness to put in a little time each week.

In the next section, we'll dive into each step in detail — with checklists, examples, and strategies you can implement immediately.

Because at the end of the day, your goal isn't just to understand AI SEO — it's to **be found by AI** so that your business can grow, your reputation can expand, and your work can reach the people who need it most.

F — Foundation: Build an Unshakable Digital Presence

The Foundation Mandate –

The primary goal of any digital strategy is stability, not just visibility. An unshakable digital presence is the non-negotiable prerequisite for enduring every algorithm shift.

In every mission I've ever led — from Special Forces operations to business ventures — the people who fail almost always skip the basics. They jump ahead to the exciting stuff and forget the groundwork.

In the Army, I watched strong, capable soldiers crumble during Special Forces selection (our "try out" process) — not because they lacked muscle or motivation, but because they hadn't mastered the fundamentals: tying a proper bowline, reading a map, or shooting accurately under pressure. They wanted the glory before they built the foundation.

Building your digital presence is exactly the same.

You can have a beautiful website, an amazing product, and the best service in town — but if your foundation isn't clear, consistent, and credible, **no one (and no AI)** will know you exist.

Your foundation is your **digital identity** — how you present yourself to the world, both to people and to machines. It's how Google, Bing, Apple, and AI systems like ChatGPT or Perplexity decide whether to trust you and recommend you.

Without a solid foundation, everything else you do in SEO or AI SEO collapses.

This is where we start.

Establishing Your Foundation

Your foundation begins with one goal: **ownership and consistency.**

You must *own your brand online* — your name, your listings, your domain, and your data — and make sure every version of it tells the same story everywhere it appears.

That means registering and verifying your business on major platforms, including:

Google Business Profile
https://www.google.com/business/

Bing Places for Business
https://www.bingplaces.com/

Apple Business Connect (Apple Maps)
https://businessconnect.apple.com/

Yelp for Business
https://biz.yelp.com/

LinkedIn Company Page
https://www.linkedin.com/company/setup/new/

Trustpilot
https://www.trustpilot.com/

Better Business Bureau
https://www.bbb.org/

Facebook Business Page
https://www.facebook.com/pages/create/

Wikidata Entry
https://www.wikidata.org/wiki/Wikidata:Main_Page

Foursquare for Business
https://foursquare.com/partners/

Each of these platforms feeds information into the broader web ecosystem.

If your **Name, Address, and Phone (NAP)** match across these profiles, AI systems will treat them as one unified identity.

If not, you'll confuse the algorithms.

It's like telling ten people ten different versions of your name — nobody knows who you really are.

Name Address Phone (NAP) Consistency
AI Trust Signal

Good

AI Recommends

Bad

AI Confused
No Recommendation

Dr. Smith's Dental Practice 123 Main Street (555) 123-1234	Website	Dr. Smith's 123 Main Street (555) 123-1234
Dr. Smith's Dental Practice 123 Main Street (555) 123-1234	Google	Dr. Smith's Dental Practice 123 Main Street (555) 987-6543
Dr. Smith's Dental Practice 123 Main Street (555) 123-1234	Yelp	Smith's DP 123 Main Street (555) 123-1234
Dr. Smith's Dental Practice 123 Main Street (555) 123-1234	Apple Maps	Smith's Dental Practice 123 Main Street Disconnected

Verifying Your Listings

When I say "verify your listings," I simply mean making sure that your business actually exists — that your email works, your phone rings, and your mail reaches you. Many directories will confirm this by sending:

A **postcard** with a code (Google and Bing do this),

A **confirmation email**, or

A **verification phone call**.

You don't need to sign up for every review platform in the world. Instead, choose one or two — for example, **Google Reviews** and **Trustpilot** — and focus on keeping them active and positive. AI systems will recognize the consistency and reward it with trust.

The Digital Breadcrumb Trail

When I say "create a digital breadcrumb trail," I mean **connecting your profiles and website together in a way that forms a clear map of your online identity.**

For example:

Your **website** should link to your Google, LinkedIn, and Yelp profiles.

Those profiles should link back to your website.

Your social media pages should use the same logo, same tagline, and same links.

When you interconnect everything, AI systems follow those "breadcrumbs" to verify that all these pages belong to the same entity — *you.*

Defining Your Direction

In Special Forces planning, we always began with the question: *What is the desired end state?* Everything else was built backward from that.

In business, your desired end state is to be **found by AI** — but you need to decide *for what.*

What do you want to be known for?

What kind of customer do you want to attract?

What expertise or value sets you apart from the rest of your industry?

This process of defining your audience and your message is known as identifying your **Ideal Customer Profile (ICP).** You'll find a specific **prompt** later in this book to help you define yours.

Once you know your ICP, every part of your online presence — your content, your language, your visuals, and your listings — should reflect that focus.

For example:

A **local bakery** might tailor its content around "fresh pastries and community events in Charleston."

A **fitness coach** might target "busy professionals over 40 who want to regain energy and confidence."

A **family-run plumbing company** might highlight "24/7 emergency service and honest pricing."

AI learns patterns.

If you consistently represent your business the same way, the system begins to *understand* what you're about — and when users ask for your type of service, it's far more likely to recommend you.

Be Clear, Be Legitimate, Be Consistent

Complexity kills clarity.

Don't try to sound bigger, fancier, or more mysterious than you are. Both humans and machines prefer the same thing — truth and simplicity.

That means no placeholder websites, no "coming soon" messages, and no confusing brand names.

Be clear about what you offer.

Be legitimate in how you present it.

Be consistent everywhere.

If you specialize in eco-friendly home cleaning, that message should appear on your website, in your Google description, in your social media bios, and even in your customer reviews. AI will see that repetition as *evidence* of expertise and authenticity.

Legitimacy also includes **digital paperwork** — verified contact information, real photos, up-to-date hours, licenses, and consistent branding.

When your business looks professional and uniform across platforms, AI systems interpret that as *trustworthy*.

The Goal of Your Foundation

Your goal is simple: **send the internet one unified signal about your identity and purpose.**

When your business name, address, phone, website, and messaging are consistent everywhere, AI systems can confidently say:

"I know who this business is. I know what they do. I trust them enough to recommend them."

That's the power of a strong foundation. It's your reputation, made visible to machines.

Once you've established it, every future layer - optimization, content, and authority - will amplify your visibility.

Real-World Example: The Two Mechanics

Let's look at two mechanics.

Mechanic A has a website but no Google Business listing. Their phone number on Yelp is disconnected, their LinkedIn company page says "under construction," and their business address is missing on Apple Maps.

Mechanic B has a verified Google Business profile, the same NAP data across all platforms, a few honest customer reviews, and photos of their shop.

When someone asks an AI assistant, *"Find the best mechanic near me,"* guess which one it recommends?

Mechanic B — every time.

Not because their wrenches are cleaner, but because their data is clearer.

AI rewards clarity. Humans do too.

Pro Tip Checklist – Foundation

Building your foundation is like setting up your headquarters. If you get this right, everything else — optimization, content, and authority — runs smoother and faster.

Here's how to establish your digital identity step-by-step.

Phase 1: Define Your Business and Brand Mission

Before you build, you must know what you're building for. This is where you define your digital identity — who you are, what you do, and who you serve.

✓ **Decide what your business *is* and what you want to be known for.**
Write a single, clear sentence that describes your service and your promise to customers.

✓ **Define your Ideal Customer Profile (ICP).**
Know exactly who you want to serve. (You'll find a guided prompt later in the book to help define your ICP.)

✓ **Clarify your Unique Value Proposition (UVP).**
What makes your product or service different from competitors? Write it down and use it everywhere.

✓ **Choose your main keywords and topics.**
What should AI and customers associate your business with?

Example: "Emergency Plumbing in Boise" or "Cybersecurity for Small Businesses."

✓ **Select a consistent business name and tagline.**
Use the same name, tagline, and brand language everywhere to reinforce credibility.

✓ **Secure your domain name.**
Purchase your business name (and close variations) using a trusted registrar like HostGator, Google Domains, Namecheap, or GoDaddy.

  o Always use **HTTPS** (secure version).

✓ **Write a short brand mission statement.**
One paragraph explaining what you stand for, who you serve, and why you exist.

  o Keep it in your About page and social media bios.

Phase 2: Register and Verify Your Business Identity

Once you've defined who you are, make sure the internet agrees with you.

✓ **Register your business on all major directories:**

- **Google Business Profile**
  https://www.google.com/business

- **Bing Places for Business**
  https://www.bingplaces.com

- **Apple Business Connect (Apple Maps)**
  https://businessconnect.apple.com

- **Yelp for Business**
  https://biz.yelp.com

- **LinkedIn Company Page**
  https://www.linkedin.com/company/setup/new

- **Trustpilot**
  https://www.trustpilot.com

- **Better Business Bureau (BBB)**
  https://www.bbb.org

- **Facebook Business Page**
  https://www.facebook.com/pages/create

- **Wikidata Entry**
  https://www.wikidata.org/wiki/Wikidata:Main Page

- **Foursquare for Business**
  https://foursquare.com/partners

✓ **Verify each listing.**

Some will send a postcard (Google, Bing), others confirm via email or phone.

Verification simply means the address, phone, and email you list actually reach you.

✓ **Maintain consistent NAP (Name – Address – Phone).**

The exact spelling and format must match on every listing. If one says "123 Main St." and another says "123 Main Street," fix it.

✓ **Upload real images.**

Show your team, workspace, and logo. Avoid generic stock photos.

✓ **Create a digital breadcrumb trail.**

Link all your listings and profiles back to your main website — and link your website to those profiles. This interconnected loop confirms that they all belong to the same verified entity — *you*.

Phase 3: Build Trust and Credibility

Trust is the invisible currency of the digital world.

Once your business exists online, show proof that you're real, active, and reputable.

✓ **Set up a review platform (choose one or two).**

- o If you're a local business: **Google Reviews** or **Trustpilot**.

- o Don't overwhelm yourself with too many review sites; consistency beats quantity.

✓ **Develop a simple customer review system.**

After each sale or service, send a short message or QR code link asking for feedback.

✓ **Respond to reviews regularly.**

Acknowledge both praise and criticism — AI recognizes responsiveness as legitimacy.

✓ **List your business hours and contact info clearly.**

Keep them updated on all profiles and your website footer.

✓ **Use the same logo, brand colors, and fonts everywhere.**

Uniform branding equals professional trust.

✓ **Add licenses, certifications, and awards** (if applicable).

These signals strengthen your credibility in both human and machine eyes.

✓ **Show your human side.**

Include short bios, photos, or mission statements about your team. AI values authentic, verifiable entities — not faceless websites.

Phase 4: Maintain, Monitor, and Adapt

The final phase of foundation work isn't glamorous, but it's what separates the amateurs from the pros.

A strong foundation needs regular checks and updates.

✓ **Audit your profiles quarterly.**

Revisit each major listing, directory, and link to ensure they're still accurate.

✓ **Test your website links.**

Make sure all your directory buttons and contact links work. Broken links erode trust.

✓ **Keep your email monitored and phone answered.**

These are digital "heartbeats" — if they go unanswered, you appear inactive.

✓ **Back up your website and data monthly.**

Prevents catastrophic loss if your host or system fails.

✓ **Stay updated on platform policies.**

Google, Yelp, and Facebook update guidelines often. Stay compliant to remain visible.

AI Search Prompts — Foundation

Below are the AI Search Prompts you can use to help AI strengthen your business foundation. Most of these prompts correspond directly with the Pro Tips, while a few (such as "register your business with the Better Business Bureau") are simple action steps that don't require a prompt.

Phase 1: Define Your Business and Brand Mission

➤ "Help me define my Ideal Customer Profile (ICP) based on my business description: [paste description]."

➤ "Write a one-sentence summary of what my business does and who it serves."

➤ "Suggest a unique value proposition that differentiates my business from competitors."

➤ "List five tagline ideas based on this mission: [paste mission]."

➤ "Recommend keyword-rich but natural domain names for my business idea."

➤ "What are 10 keyword phrases AI systems might associate with my business type?"

Phase 2: Register and Verify Your Business Identity

➤ "Which directories matter most for my specific industry?"

➤ "Should I register on both Trustpilot and Google Reviews, or focus on one?"

➤ "What information should my Google Business Profile include for maximum AI impact?"

➤ "Check this NAP for consistency: [paste business name, address, phone]."

➤ "Generate a 75-word business description with my primary keyword."

Phase 3: Build Trust and Credibility

➤ "Write a customer follow-up message asking politely for a Google or Trustpilot review."

➤ "Suggest five ways to humanize my brand online without showing my face."

➤ "List professional certifications or associations that would build credibility in [industry]."

➤ "Draft a 100-word 'About Us' paragraph including location and service keywords."

➤ "How should I respond professionally to a negative online review?"

Phase 4: Maintain, Monitor, and Adapt

➤ "Create a quarterly digital audit checklist for my business listings and website."

➤ "Suggest tools to alert me if my business name or reviews change online."

➢ "Generate a 12-month reminder calendar for content, reviews, and audits."

➢ "Write a short SOP for updating my business listings."

➢ "Recommend automation tools to monitor broken links or downtime."

Closing Reflection

A strong foundation doesn't just make your business discoverable — it makes it unshakable. The businesses that endure won't be the fastest or the flashiest; they'll be the ones that built solid systems before they needed them. Your digital foundation is no different. It's your proof of life in the AI era — your signal to the world that says, "I exist, I'm real, and I can be trusted." Once that signal is steady, everything else — optimization, content, and authority — amplifies it.

Key Takeaways

AI systems reward clarity, consistency, and credibility — not complexity.

A verified, interconnected digital footprint proves you're real and trustworthy.

Reviews, real photos, and consistent NAP data are modern trust signals.

Quarterly audits prevent decay and keep your foundation current.

Once your foundation is solid, AI can finally see you — and recommend you.

Now that you've secured yours, it's time to move into the next section: **O — Optimization**, where we'll show you how to make your content machine-readable so AI systems can truly understand and recommend you.

O — Optimization: Make Your Message Machine-Readable

> **Machine Trust Doctrine -**
>
> AI trusts clarity, not complexity. If a generative engine cannot easily parse, fact-check, and cite your content, it will not recommend your authority to its users.

I learned about Optimization the hard way.

When I first started writing online, I thought, *"if my content is good, people will find it."*

I had written deep, thoughtful articles — some of them took days. But when I searched for them on Google... nothing. They were invisible. It was like shouting into an empty canyon.

It reminded me of that old question: *If a tree falls in the forest and no one hears it, did it make a sound?* You could have the cure for cancer bottled up in your garage, but if nobody can find it, it might as well not exist.

That's what this chapter is about — **how to make your content findable, readable, and understandable by machines.**

Because today, the gatekeepers aren't just human readers. They're algorithms. AI assistants. Search bots. If they can't read you, they can't recommend you.

Optimization isn't about "tricking Google." It's about **translating your brilliance into a language that machines understand** — so that real people can discover you.

Optimization

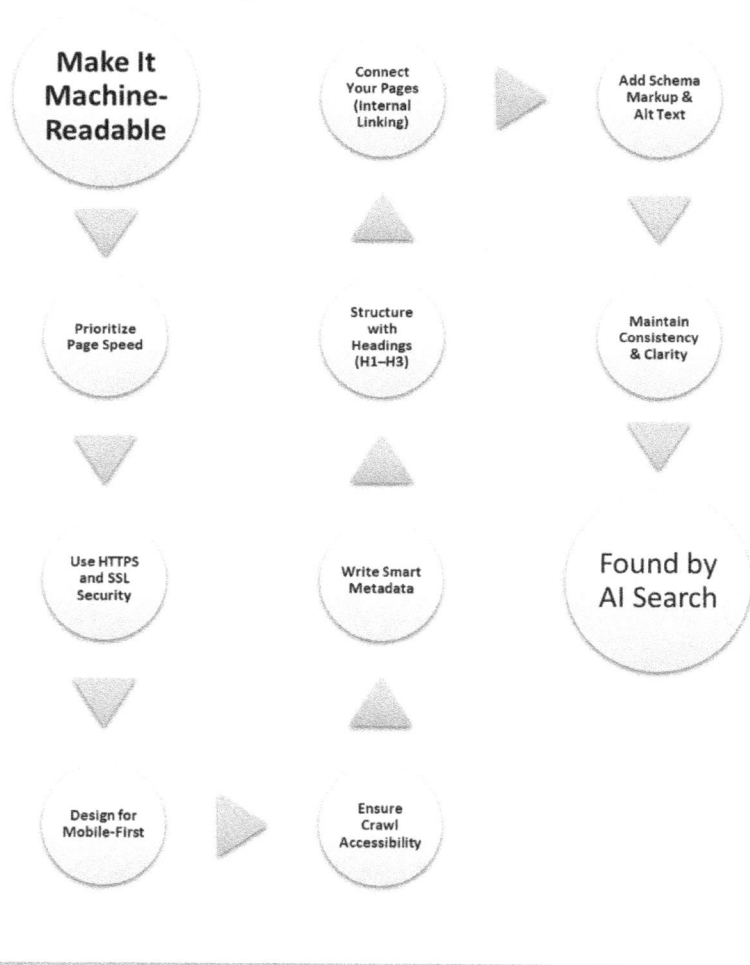

Make It Machine-Readable

Connect Your Pages (Internal Linking)

Add Schema Markup & Alt Text

Prioritize Page Speed

Structure with Headings (H1–H3)

Maintain Consistency & Clarity

Use HTTPS and SSL Security

Write Smart Metadata

Found by AI Search

Design for Mobile-First

Ensure Crawl Accessibility

Why Machine Readability Matters

Humans can guess your meaning. Machines can't. You and I can read a confusing paragraph and still get the point.

AI systems don't guess — they *parse*.

Think of AI like a diligent librarian who has to decide where to shelve every book in the world.

If your "book" (your webpage) doesn't have a clear title, chapter headings, or topic summary, that librarian has no idea where to file it. Your "book" disappears into the back room — indexed, maybe, but never surfaced.

When you optimize for machine understanding, you're giving that librarian:

➢ a clear cover title (meta title),

➢ an inside summary (meta description),

➢ a chapter outline (H1s, H2s, H3s),

➢ and references (internal and external links).

Machines crave structure and context.

And when you provide both, you're rewarded — with visibility.

Technical SEO Basics

This isn't about coding or advanced tools.

It's about knowing what matters, why it matters, and what to check.

Let's go step-by-step through the essentials.

Page Speed: Be Fast or Be Forgotten

People hate waiting, and so do algorithms.

A slow site tells both the user and the machine, "We don't value your time."

Compress your images (convert to WebP), use a content delivery network (CDN) if you can, and keep fancy animations minimal.

Fast sites are seen as competent, professional, and trustworthy.

You can check your site's speed at https://pagespeed.web.dev.

SSL / HTTPS (The Lock Icon)

You've seen the little lock symbol in the top-left of your browser — right next to a website's URL.

That's called **SSL,** or **Secure Sockets Layer**, and it ensures that data sent between the user's computer and your site stays encrypted and safe.

If your website starts with **https://** (note the "s"), that means you're secure.

If it only starts with **http://**, you're missing it — and most browsers will flag your site as "Not Secure."

How to get it:

Most modern hosting providers (like SiteGround, Bluehost, or GoDaddy) include a free SSL certificate through **Let's Encrypt.**

If not, you can enable one with a few clicks inside your hosting control panel. Once installed, always redirect all traffic from http → https.

This small step tells both humans and search engines: "You can trust me."

Mobile-First Design

More than 60% of all web traffic now comes from phones. If your site looks perfect on desktop but broken on mobile, you're losing customers — and ranking points.

A **mobile-first** website automatically adjusts its layout to fit smaller screens.

Buttons are easy to tap, text is readable without zooming, and images resize correctly.

You can check how your site looks on mobile using your phone or the **Inspect → Mobile View** feature in Chrome.

If your readers can't use your site on mobile, AI and search engines won't recommend it.

Crawl Accessibility: Let The Bots In

Search engines don't "see" your site like humans do.

They **crawl** it — meaning small computer programs called *bots* or *spiders* visit your pages, follow your links, and learn what your site is about.

To make sure they can do that, two files matter most:

1. robots.txt

This file tells search bots which pages they can or can't visit. For example, you might block private pages like "/checkout/" or "/admin/" but allow everything else.

In WordPress, SEO plugins like **Yoast** or **Rank Math** automatically create and manage this file for you. You can check yours by typing this into your browser:

yourdomain.com/robots.txt

If it says "Disallow: /", that means bots are blocked from everything (bad).

If it lists certain folders but allows most, that's fine.

2. XML Sitemap

Think of a sitemap like a table of contents for your website. It lists every important page and tells bots, "Here's what matters."

Yoast and RankMath both generate this automatically. You can find yours at:

yourdomain.com/sitemap_index.xml

Once you have it, submit it inside **Google Search Console** and **Bing Webmaster Tools** so the search engines can crawl you efficiently.

Meta Titles, Descriptions, and URL Slugs

Every time you create a new page or blog post, your website asks you for a few things:

Title: what your page is called

Description: a short summary of what it's about

Slug: the part of the URL after the slash (like "/contact" or "/boise-plumbing")

Keywords: optional, but Yoast helps guide you here

Here's what they mean:

Meta Title: This is the big blue link people see in search results. Keep it under 60 characters.

Example: *Emergency Plumbing in Boise | Smith Plumbing*

Meta Description: The short gray text underneath. Keep it under 160 characters and make it human.

Example: *Need 24/7 plumbing help in Boise? Call Smith Plumbing for fast, affordable service.*

URL Slug: The web address after your domain. Keep it short, lowercase, and separated by hyphens.

Example: /boise-emergency-plumbing

These three fields are your storefront sign, your slogan, and your street address — don't skip them.

If you use **Yoast**, it will prompt you to fill these out under each page or post. It also gives you a "green light" when it's optimized.

Headings (H1, H2, H3)

Headings are not decorations — they're structure.

If your page were a book, the **H1** is your title, the **H2s** are your chapters, and the **H3s** are your subpoints.

Rules of thumb:

Use **one H1 per page.** It's the main topic.

Use **H2s** to divide sections.

Use **H3s** for smaller points under each H2.

Don't skip from H1 straight to H4. Keep hierarchy logical.

This helps both readers and machines know what each section covers — and whether your content answers their question.

Example:

H1: Emergency Plumbing in Boise

H2: Why Choose Smith Plumbing

H3: Certified, Local, and Family-Owned

H2: Services We Offer

H3: Drain Cleaning

H3: Water Heater Repairs

Internal Linking

Internal linking simply means linking your pages to each other. If your "Services" page mentions "water heater installation," link that phrase to your dedicated "Water Heater Installation" page.

It's like creating trails between campsites on a map. Bots follow those trails to understand your site's structure and topic relationships.

Example:

A bakery links "birthday cakes" → "custom cakes" → "wedding cakes."

A realtor links "homes for sale in Miami" → "Miami condo guide" → "mortgage calculator."

This helps users explore more and tells AI that you're a connected, credible authority in your niche.

Canonical Tags (Avoid Duplicate Confusion)

Sometimes you'll have similar or duplicate pages — like /product and /product? ref=ad123.

Search engines can get confused, thinking they're two separate pages.

A **canonical tag** tells them, "These are the same; index this one."

Yoast automatically handles this by marking the main version of each page as the canonical.

You can check by viewing your page's source (right-click → View Page Source → search for "canonical").

If you see <link rel="canonical" href="https://yourdomain.com/main-page/" />, you're good.

Alt Text for Images

Every time you upload an image, you'll see several fields:

File name

Title

Caption

Alt text

The **alt text** is the most important for SEO. It's what machines read when they can't "see" an image.

Example:

Weak alt text: "IMG_0021"

Strong alt text: "Technician installing tankless water heater in Boise home."

Alt text helps AI understand what's in the image and builds credibility (Experience & Expertise in E-E-A-T). It also makes your site accessible to people using screen readers.

Schema Markup (Structured Data)

Schema is like a secret code for search engines.

It's small bits of text (usually in **JSON-LD**, a format of structured data written in JavaScript Object Notation) that tell AI *exactly* what your page represents.

Example:

A normal human might read:

"John's Auto Repair. We fix brakes, engines, and transmissions. Call (555) 123-4567."

But an AI reads the schema and learns:

```
{
"@context": "https://schema.org",
"@type": "AutoRepair",
"name": "John's Auto Repair",
"address": {
"@type": "PostalAddress",
"streetAddress": "123 Main Street",
"addressLocality": "Boise",
"addressRegion": "ID",
"postalCode": "83701"
},
"telephone": "(555) 123-4567",
"openingHours": "Mo-Fr 08:00-17:00"
}
```

That's what helps AI verify your business identity across the internet.

Many plugins (Yoast, RankMath, All-in-One SEO) add basic schema automatically.

But for advanced setups — like products, FAQs, or How-To articles — you can add extra schema manually at the bottom of your page.

Schema Reminder:

We'll include a "Build Schema" prompt at the end of this book so you can safely generate custom code without breaking anything.

How Machines Read and Rank Your Page

Here's what happens behind the scenes when someone searches:

A crawler (bot) visits your page.

It checks your robots. txt to see if it's allowed in.

It follows your sitemap to discover related pages.

It scans your headings, titles, schema, and links to understand the topic.

It indexes your content — adding it to a massive library of the web.

When a user or AI asks a question, the system predicts which pages best fit the meaning, not just the words.

If your structure is clear, your identity consistent, and your topic coverage strong, your chances of inclusion skyrocket.

A Real-World Before and After

Let's do a quick real-world example.

Here's what *wrong* looks like, and then I'll show you *right*.

Before (weak):

Title: "Home"

H1: "Welcome to Our Site"

URL: /index. php? p=1

Body: "We do everything. Call us."

After (strong):

Title: "Emergency Plumbing in Boise | Smith Plumbing — 24/7 Service"

H1: "Emergency Plumbing in Boise"

URL: /boise-emergency-plumbing

Body: Starts with a TL;DR, has clear H2s ("Our Services," "Why Choose Us," "FAQ"), interlinks to related pages ("Water Heater Repair"), and includes Local Business + FAQ schema.

Footer lists NAP (Name, Address, Phone).

Images include real photos with alt text.

Page loads fast on mobile and passes Core Web Vitals.

The first example disappears into the noise.

The second gets read, ranked, and cited — because it's clear.

Pro Tip Checklist – Optimization

Optimization is an ongoing discipline, not a one-time setup.

To make it manageable, I recommend that you break "Optimization" into two categories:

1. **Pro Tips for Your Entire Website** – foundational setup tasks that affect every page.
2. **Pro Tips for Each Page or Blog Article** – repeatable actions for every piece of content you publish.

Each layer strengthens the one before it. Begin with the full-website setup, then move into individual optimization.

Pro Tips for Your Entire Website

✓ **Enable HTTPS (secure connection).**

Confirm that your site loads as **https://** instead of **http://**. Activate a free SSL certificate through your hosting provider or Let's Encrypt, and redirect all non-secure URLs to secure ones.

✓ **Create and submit an XML sitemap.**

Most SEO plugins like Yoast or Rank Math generate this automatically. You can usually find it at *yourdomain.com/sitemap_index.xml*. Submit the sitemap to **Google Search Console** and **Bing Webmaster Tools**.

✓ **Check your robots. txt file.**

Visit *yourdomain.com/robots.txt* to ensure it isn't blocking key pages. A "Disallow: /" line can prevent your entire site from being indexed. Yoast manages this automatically, but it's worth confirming manually.

✓ **Add your business NAP (Name – Address – Phone).**

Include this information in your website footer and on your Contact page. Make sure it matches exactly with your listings on Google, Bing, Apple, and Yelp.

✓ **Activate Core Web Vitals tracking.**

Run a test at **pagespeed.web.dev**. Address any red flags in performance, accessibility, or best practices to improve speed and user experience.

✓ **Design mobile-first.**

Preview your website on multiple phones and tablets. Check that text is readable, buttons are easy to tap, and layout shifts are minimal.

✓ **Enable schema automation.**

Confirm that your SEO plugin (Yoast or Rank Math) has schema enabled by default. If not, plan to add JSON-LD manually later using the provided prompt in this book.

✓ **Secure your brand identity.**

Use the same logo, tagline, and tone of voice across your website and social media channels. Consistency helps AI verify that all your properties belong to the same entity.

✓ **Audit quarterly.**

Every three months, recheck your robots.txt, sitemap, page speed, and schema to ensure nothing has silently broken in the background.

Pro Tips for Each Page or Blog Article

✓ **Set a meta title (under 60 characters).**

Include your main keyword and brand name. Example: *Emergency Plumbing in Boise | Smith Plumbing.*

✓ **Write a meta description (under 160 characters).**

Summarize the page's benefit in plain English. Example: *24/7 Boise plumbers for leaks, clogs, and emergencies.*

✓ **Use a clean URL slug.**

Keep it short, lowercase, and hyphenated. Example: */boise-emergency-plumbing.*

✓ **Include one H1 heading per page.**

Your H1 should clearly describe the topic of the page or article.

✓ **Organize with H2 and H3 subheadings.**

Think of H2s as section headers and H3s as supporting points. They help both humans and AI understand structure.

✓ **Add a TL;DR summary at the top.**

Write two to four sentences summarizing what the page delivers. Both AI systems and readers appreciate a quick overview.

✓ **End with a Key Takeaways box.**

This reinforces clarity and makes your content more likely to appear in AI summaries and snippets.

✓ **Add two to four internal links.**

Connect relevant pages using descriptive anchor text. Example: *Learn more about our water heater services.*

✓ **Optimize every image.**

Rename image files with descriptive keywords (e. g., *boise-water-heater.webp*). Add alt text that explains what's shown in natural language. Example: *Technician installing a new water heater in a Boise home.*

✓ **Add canonical tags to avoid duplicates.**

Yoast handles this automatically, but verify that each page specifies its "official" version.

✓ **Add schema markup.**

Include Local Business, Product, Service, or FAQ schema depending on the page type. Plugin-generated schema works, but custom JSON-LD provides better precision.

✓ **Check page speed before publishing.**

Compress large images, enable caching, and use a performance-friendly host to ensure quick loading.

✓ **Test every page on mobile.**

Use your actual phone, not just a desktop simulator. Verify that everything displays properly without zooming or broken elements.

✓ **Add contact information in the footer.**

This reinforces legitimacy and makes it easy for customers to reach you.

✓ **Verify all internal and external links.**

Fix broken ones and update outdated references once a year.

✓ **FAQs for blog articles:**

Add a short FAQ section with three to eight real customer questions and answers. Mark it up with JSON-LD using your SEO plugin. Include Article and Author schema, refresh content annually with new data, and monitor analytics for engagement and topic relevance.

✓ **Verify that Your Page is Indexed (Visible):**

If your pages aren't appearing in Google results, check Google Search Console. It will often show "Crawled – Not Indexed" or "Blocked by robots. txt," which tells you exactly what's wrong.

AI Search Prompts — Optimization

Below are the AI Search Prompts you can use to help AI optimize your website and content for machine understanding.

Website-Wide Prompts

➢ "Analyze my website's Core Web Vitals and suggest 5 improvements."
➢ "Check my robots.txt and sitemap structure for SEO issues."
➢ "Generate JSON-LD schema for my business type: [describe business]."
➢ "Suggest ways to improve mobile readability for my homepage."
➢ "Audit my site branding for consistency across all pages."

Page & Blog Prompts

- ➢ "Write a meta title and description for this page: [paste text]."
- ➢ "Generate a TL;DR summary and three Key Takeaways for this article."
- ➢ "Suggest internal linking opportunities between these pages: [list URLs]."
- ➢ "Write FAQ schema with 3 questions and answers about [topic]."
- ➢ "Optimize alt text for the following images: [describe or list filenames]."
- ➢ "Generate canonical tags and schema recommendations for this page."

Closing Reflections

Optimization is precision communication.

You're not tricking machines — you're teaching them how to read you. Every line of code, every title tag, and every schema snippet is a signal of clarity and credibility.

When your structure speaks the same language as AI, your content becomes effortless to understand and easy to recommend.

That's not manipulation — it's mastery.

Key Takeaways

Machines don't reward mystery; they reward clarity.

A fast, mobile-friendly, and schema-rich website builds trust.

Every page and post should explain one idea clearly and link naturally.

Consistency in structure equals credibility in AI eyes.

Optimization isn't about chasing algorithms — it's about communicating truth with precision.

Now that your digital architecture is optimized for comprehension, it's time to shift focus to **Utility — creating content that solves human problems.** Because the best SEO signal of all is being genuinely useful.

U — Utility: Create Content That Solves Human Problems

The Customer Principle -

Content that fails to resolve a user's fundamental need is digital noise. Value is the single metric that guarantees human engagement and long-term conversion.

Utility begins with having a good product — one that's genuinely useful.

If your product stinks, it doesn't matter how clever your SEO is — people are going to figure it out. They'll discover that your product or service is below average, your reviews will reflect it, and your reputation will slowly crash and burn.

But when you have both a great product *and* great AI SEO, you start a positive spiral: customers find you, they're genuinely helped, and they tell others. Each good experience reinforces your visibility.

We've all clicked on a promising link that looked like it would answer our question — only to find the page full of fluff, filler, and keywords. It was obviously written by someone who wanted a click, not someone who cared about helping us. That's the old way.

In the age of AI search, you can't fake usefulness. It's not about gaming the system anymore. It's about being the most helpful answer to a real human problem.

Old SEO rewarded keyword density.

AI SEO rewards clarity, credibility, and *helpfulness*.

If you want to rise in this new ecosystem, don't chase clicks — **solve problems.**

Why This Matters Now

Every person who finds your website arrives with a simple, unspoken question: *"Can you help me?"*

They don't want to be impressed. They want relief — an answer, a path, a next step. If your content gives them that, they'll stay, they'll trust you, and they'll remember you.

AI systems measure these signals. When humans stay longer, share links, and interact more, AI interprets that as proof of value. So, by being **useful for humans first**, you automatically become favored by AI systems.

The Core Idea: Be the Most Helpful Answer

Usefulness isn't a buzzword — it's a mindset.

It means creating content that genuinely helps people by being clear, complete, and easy to act on. When both humans and AI systems visit your page, they should instantly understand the problem you solve, the steps you recommend, and why you can be trusted to give the answer.

To become the most helpful answer, build each page or post around these eight core elements:

➤ **TL;DR Summary (Too Long; Didn't Read)** – A short, two- to five-line summary that gives the main answer right at the top of your page. It's a quick orientation for busy readers and AI systems alike, helping them understand what your content delivers before they read the details. Think of it as your mission briefing — fast, focused, and outcome-driven.

➤ **Problem in Plain English** – State the issue your audience is facing in simple, conversational language. When you show you understand what frustrates them, they're more likely to trust your guidance.

➤ **Proof of Experience (E-E-A-T: Experience, Expertise, Authoritativeness, and Trustworthiness)** – Demonstrate that you've lived what you teach. Share short personal stories, professional results, or real-world lessons learned. This signals to both people and algorithms that your advice is credible, tested, and worth trusting.

➤ **Definitions and Formulas** – Whenever you use technical terms, acronyms, or calculations, define them in plain English. Explaining complex ideas simply doesn't weaken your authority — it strengthens it by making your knowledge accessible.

➤ **Step-by-Step Help** – Offer a clear sequence of actions or numbered instructions that walk the reader through the solution. This reduces confusion and builds confidence.

➤ **FAQ Section (Frequently Asked Questions)** – Include real questions your customers or readers ask most often. This shows empathy, anticipates uncertainty, and helps AI systems recognize that your page provides comprehensive, relevant answers.

➤ **Downloadable Tools** – Offer something your audience can use immediately, such as a checklist, calculator, or template. Practical tools turn good advice into real-world value.

➤ **Next Step CTA (Call-to-Action)** – End each piece of content with clarity about what the reader should do next. Whether it's reading a related article, downloading a resource, or contacting your business, a clear call-to-action transforms understanding into measurable results.

Becoming the most helpful answer isn't about writing the most words — it's about solving someone's problem as quickly, clearly, and confidently as possible. When your content truly helps, both humans and AI will recognize your value — and reward it.

AI Rewards Helpful Answers

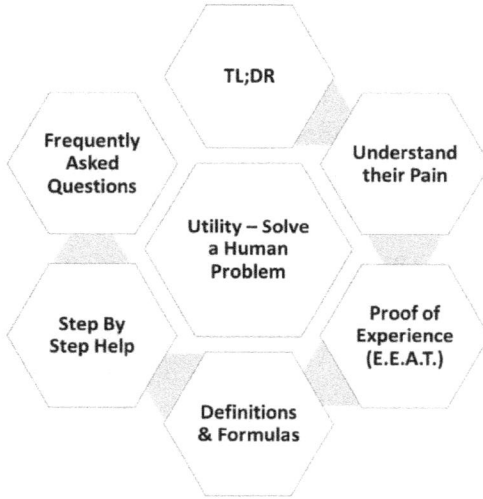

TL;DR

Frequently Asked Questions

Understand their Pain

Utility – Solve a Human Problem

Step By Step Help

Proof of Experience (E.E.A.T.)

Definitions & Formulas

Conversational Writing and Clarity

Your content should sound like you're helping a friend, not lecturing a stranger.

The most effective pages are written in a warm, conversational tone that combines empathy with authority.

Start by writing as if you're answering a specific person's question. Use **"you," "we," and "let's."** Avoid the third-person detachment of corporate copy.

Break ideas into short paragraphs. Use lists. Add bold highlights where the eye needs to pause. Humans scan; machines parse. You serve both by keeping structure simple.

Here's a useful pattern:

Begin with a brief story or scenario that shows you understand the reader's pain.

Clarify the problem in plain English.

Offer the steps to fix it.

Reassure them with a sentence like, "You're not the only one who's struggled with this — here's what to do next."

And whenever you introduce a new term, define it immediately.

For example: **Cognitive Load**

Cognitive load is the mental weight people carry when trying to understand something new. The heavier that load, the quicker they give up.

When your writing is clear — when ideas are structured logically, definitions appear the moment they're needed, and paragraphs breathe — you lighten that load. The result is instant trust.

It's the same reason great teachers, great leaders, and great products feel effortless: they hide the hard work behind simplicity.

Your readers shouldn't have to struggle to learn from you. They should glide through the page, nodding as they go, thinking, "Finally — someone who gets it."

That's the essence of utility: making the complex feel simple, and the valuable feel easy to grasp.

Writing that's conversational and clear does more than make your readers comfortable — it keeps them learning. And when people learn something from you, they begin to trust you.

That's usefulness in action.

Human – AI Collaboration in Content Creation

AI can help you write faster, but it can't help you *care more*. That part is on you.

In my own workflow, I use AI as a collaborator — not a ghostwriter. Here's how:

I give AI a clear prompt outlining the topic, tone, and goal.

AI produces a first draft — sometimes good, sometimes clunky.

I record my edits, voice notes, or critiques — explaining what works and what doesn't.

I upload that feedback back to the AI and let it produce a refined second version.

Finally, I re-edit and add *true stories from my life or field experience* to ground the message in authenticity.

This process keeps the writing efficient yet deeply personal. The AI helps with structure, grammar, and speed — but the voice, judgment, and truth are human.

That's the future of authentic, scalable content: **Human-in-the-Loop creation.**

Machines generate; humans validate, refine, and personalize.

Topical Depth and Quality

Usefulness is depth. The web doesn't need more surface-level "10 Tips for Success." It needs expertise that builds understanding.

Build Deep Content Ecosystems

Think of your site as a connected library, not a list of posts. Choose cornerstone topics that represent your core expertise and link every related subtopic back to them.

Example: "The Ultimate Guide to Home Cybersecurity" might anchor subtopics like "Best Password Managers," "How to Secure Your Wi-Fi," and "VPN Myths."

This cluster signals to both readers and AI that you own this subject.

Update Cornerstone Pieces Annually

A stale page is a broken promise. Schedule a yearly refresh for your major guides. Update stats, screenshots, and FAQs. Add a "Reviewed on [month/year]" line at the bottom so readers know it's current.

Use Multi-Format Storytelling

Different people learn in different ways. Some read, some watch, some listen. Serve them all.

- Text explains.
- Images demonstrate.
- Audio comforts.
- Video proves.

Add at least two formats per key topic. A 3-minute explainer video, an infographic, or even a short audio clip can multiply your usefulness.

Multi-format content increases engagement, comprehension, and trust — and it gives AI richer context to understand your expertise.

Timely or Timeless — Choosing Your AI Visibility Strategy

Beyond rewarding utility and helpfulness, AI search rewards two other virtues: **speed** and **stability**.

If your world moves fast — tech, news, investing, travel, or politics — AI engines that summarize reality prefer **recency**. They reference what's being talked about *right now*. That means writing something the same night or morning after a major development can earn you a **supersized share of visibility**. Timely content often becomes the first citation AI systems see — and once they quote it, they tend to repeat it. In the world of digital visibility, *first often beats perfect*.

But not every business lives on headlines. If you provide **evergreen services** — law, accounting, construction, cybersecurity, real estate — the smarter strategy is to cultivate **timeless authority**. Instead of chasing the moment, you anchor yourself as the enduring expert. Create resources that stay relevant for years, refresh them periodically, and maintain a consistent, verifiable presence across your site and platforms. You're not competing for this week's spike in attention; you're building the bedrock that AI will cite as *trustworthy and permanent*.

The best businesses balance both. They publish **timely commentary** when something relevant breaks — and reinforce it with **timeless guides** that never expire. The goal is simple: when people (or machines) ask, *"Who knows this subject best?"* the answer should always be **you**.

Case Study: The Useful Fitness Coach

A fitness coach in Austin had written dozens of articles about workouts, but none were ranking. They weren't bad — they were just generic. Nothing unique, nothing personal.

We rebuilt one flagship article titled **"How to Regain Energy and Confidence After 40."**

Here's what changed:

A **TL;DR** summary: "You don't need supplements — you need sleep, protein, and movement you enjoy."

A plain-language intro: "You're tired, busy, and your body doesn't respond like it used to."

A **7-step checklist**: hydrate, lift 3× weekly, eat 120 grams of protein, track energy not weight, etc.

A **Definitions Box**: VO_2 Max, protein timing, active recovery — all explained in one line.

A **Downloadable PDF**: "7-Day Energy Reset Plan."

A **Short Video** demonstration of mobility drills.

A **FAQ** section with questions like "Can I start if I haven't trained in years?"

He also added a 2-sentence story from his life about training exhausted parents who rediscovered confidence through consistency.

The result?

Visitors stayed six times longer. Downloads tripled. And AI assistants started referencing his guide when users asked:

"How can I boost my energy after 40 without supplements?"

That's usefulness — rooted in real empathy and lived experience.

Action Steps / Quick Wins

Add a **TL;DR** and short **FAQs** to your top 5 pages.

Turn your most-visited post into a **step-by-step guide** with a downloadable checklist.

Create a **Definitions & Formulas** box for every technical topic you cover.

Record a short **video or audio summary** for your cornerstone post.

Include a **Reviewed on [month/year]** date stamp for transparency.

End every article with a clear, natural **call to action**.

Add one short, personal **"From the Field"** story per topic.

Pro Tips Checklist — Utility

✓ **Make it instantly helpful.**

Start with a clear TL;DR summary that gives the main answer up front. Define the reader's problem in plain English, and use numbered steps with short, simple verbs. Add time, cost, or skill-level tags for each step to set expectations, and whenever possible, include a downloadable checklist or worksheet.

✓ **Create multi-layered understanding.**

Add a short Definitions Box for every piece of jargon. Include at least one formula or visual example that explains a key concept, and consider a "myth vs. fact" element to correct common misconceptions. Keep paragraphs short and use white space generously to make your writing feel open and easy to follow.

✓ **Blend empathy with expertise (E-E-A-T: Experience, Expertise, Authoritativeness, and Trustworthiness).**

Add a short "From the Field" note or a relevant photo that illustrates authenticity. Show your face or your voice in at least one format — video, podcast, or author bio —

to make your expertise relatable. Mention credentials naturally, not boastfully, and acknowledge what's not included in your guide; transparency builds trust.

✓ **Teach with FAQs and tools.**

Use real questions from your clients or audience emails. Keep each answer under five sentences, and add FAQ schema so AI systems can read and display them accurately. When possible, offer a simple calculator, estimator, or downloadable tool to make your guidance immediately actionable.

✓ **Build depth and storytelling.**

Organize your content into topic clusters that support cornerstone guides. Each major topic should connect to related subtopics, creating a web of understanding. Include at least two content formats (such as video or infographic) for each cornerstone piece, and refresh those main articles annually to keep them current and authoritative.

✓ **Win the Moment, Own the Decade**

Timeliness content creates discovery; timelessness creates authority. Fast content earns mentions, but evergreen content earns memory. Make sure your content calendar includes both — short, reactionary posts that catch AI attention *now*, and long-form, foundational pieces that ensure AI keeps finding you *later*.

AI Search Prompts — Utility

Below are the AI Search Prompts you can use to help AI make your content more useful, human-centered, and complete. Most of these prompts correspond directly with the Pro Tips, while a few focus on tone and storytelling.

➢ "Convert this article into a human-help guide with a TL;DR, problem statement, 7-step process, Definitions box, FAQ (5 Q & As), and a clear call-to-action."

➢ "Write a Definitions & Formulas box for [topic]. Include 5 terms, 1 formula, and 1 real-world example."

➢ "Generate 6 realistic FAQs for [service]. Keep answers conversational and under 80 words."

➢ "Create a 1-page checklist (PDF-ready) mirroring this 7-step process."

➢ "Propose a simple calculator idea (inputs, formula, output) for this page."

➢ "Rewrite this article in an empathetic, conversational tone that sounds human and authentic."

➢ "Suggest two alternate content formats (video or audio) to repurpose this post."

➢ "Add a short 'From the Field' paragraph to illustrate experience and credibility."

➢ "Write a short post reacting to today's [industry event/news] that explains what it means for [my target audience]. Use clear, factual language so AI systems can cite it accurately."

Closing Reflections

Every algorithm ultimately serves the same master: the human searcher.

AI doesn't reward clickbait; it rewards satisfaction. When your content makes someone say, "Finally — someone explained it clearly," you've done more for your business than any keyword ever could.

Utility is empathy in motion. It's your expertise transformed into clarity, comfort, and confidence for others.

When you help humans win, AI learns that you deserve to be found.

Key Takeaways

Write for humans first; algorithms follow.

Clarity, empathy, and real solutions are the strongest SEO signals.

Every question answered clearly strengthens both your brand and your AI visibility.

Helpful content builds loyalty, while manipulative content erodes it.

The more useful your page becomes, the more AI systems will surface it as the best answer.

Now that your content is genuinely useful, it's time to focus on Niche Authority — becoming the go-to expert in your specific field. Because once AI knows you're trustworthy and specialized, it starts recommending you more often than anyone else.

N — Niche Authority: Establish Unquestionable Expertise

> **Expertise Lock-in -**
>
> True authority is singular and defensible. You must strive to be the definitive source in your niche so that AI is forced to cite your expertise.

The Quiet Professional — Authority Without Self-Promotion

In Special Forces, there's a code we live by: *Be a Quiet Professional.*

It means you don't talk about what you've done — you let your results speak for themselves. You don't need to tell people you're the expert; your performance proves it.

Even though your reputation precedes you, people can also see what you've done right on your uniform. This guy has a combat patch. That one has a Combat Infantryman's Badge. Another wears a Purple Heart, which means he was injured in combat. Someone else has a Bronze Star with a "V" for valor. Another has a Silver Star.

Nobody walks into a new unit and announces, *"Hey, by the way, I've got a Bronze Star."* They don't have to. They work hard.

They're dependable. They're the teammate everyone wants. And once or twice a year, when the dress uniform comes out, those badges and awards tell the story quietly. No one is surprised — the uniform simply confirms their competence and credibility.

The digital world works the same way. Your online footprint — your content, reviews, and mentions — are the ribbons on your digital uniform. You don't need to brag; the record speaks for itself. True niche authority is built by quiet, visible competence and consistent contribution over time.

Goal of Niche Authority

Niche Authority means becoming the go-to expert in your field — someone trusted by both humans and machines.

Niche Authority isn't about being known by everyone. It's about being *undeniable* to the people who matter most: your audience, your customers, and your peers.

AI systems are designed to identify credible voices within topics. They notice patterns like:

➤ Consistent language and expertise across platforms.

➤ Mentions and citations from reputable sources.

➤ Evidence of real-world experience (E-E-A-T).

➤ Positive reputation signals from other humans.

➤ Authority is not declared; it's demonstrated.

Establish Authority Through Credibility

Credibility is the foundation of authority. You build it by proving — not claiming — your competence.

Earn **customer reviews and testimonials** that describe results, not just praise.

Showcase **case studies** that walk readers through the challenge, your process, and the outcome.

Display **certifications and partnerships** with credible organizations.

Maintain a verifiable **track record** — include dates, photos, or measurable metrics.

Every piece of evidence sends a signal. When AI cross-checks your online footprint, it looks for patterns that confirm you're real, consistent, and trusted by others.

Mentions, Backlinks, and Citations

In the old days, backlinks were everything. But in the world of AI-driven search, *mentions* — the mere appearance of your name or brand in credible places — are becoming just as powerful, and sometimes more so.

Here's the difference:

➢ **Keyword:** A word or phrase someone types into Google or an AI chat.
  Still important for discoverability, but also easily manipulated.

➢ **Backlink:** A clickable link from another website to yours.
  Validates your authority, strengthens SEO, and tells AI that others trust you.

➢ **Mention:** Any reference to your name, brand, or website — even if there's no hyperlink.
  Boosts visibility and teaches AI systems to associate your name with your niche and expertise.

AI models read context, not just links. If your name appears frequently in relevant conversations — articles, podcasts, interviews, Reddit threads, or directories — AI recognizes that as topical relevance.

Mentions are the New Backlinks.

They show that you're part of the conversation, not just pointing to it.

Ten Ways to Earn Mentions:

➤ Be interviewed on podcasts related to your niche.

➤ Contribute guest articles to reputable blogs.

➤ Answer expert roundups and press requests.

➤ Submit quotes through journalist platforms like **Help a Reporter Out (HARO)** or **Featured.com**.

➤ Get listed in **"best of" directories** or comparison articles.

➤ Publish helpful answers on **Quora** and **Reddit** (non-promotional).

➤ Collaborate with other experts on joint resources or webinars.

➤ Share original insights on **LinkedIn** — tag other professionals.

➤ Post your knowledge on **Medium, Substack**, or **industry forums**.

➤ Be referenced in **Wikidata** or **Wikipedia** (verifiable citations).

Each mention becomes a signal to AI that you're a credible, active voice in your field.

Backlink Sources

Every industry has its own places where backlinks can be earned. Think it through strategically, and use one of the prompts below to ask AI for a list of **the best backlink opportunities in your specific niche**.

Once you have four or five recommendations, use a simple Chrome tool to evaluate their quality.

Here are a few reliable backlink sources to get started:

➢ **AlternativeTo. net:** Create a free listing if you provide software or tools.

➢ **Sources of Sources:** A journalist database connecting experts to media outlets.

➢ **Help a Reporter Out (HARO):** Submit expert quotes for journalists.

➢ **Featured.com:** Similar to HARO, focused on professional visibility.

➢ **Free Local Directories:** Google, Bing, Yelp, Apple, and BBB remain key.

➢ **Guest Posts:** Search Google for:
"Your Niche" + "Write for Us" or "Your Niche" + "Guest Post"
Then check the "Domain Authority" of those websites. You can check a website's domain authority for free using tools like Moz's Domain Authority checker, Ahrefs' Free Domain Rating Checker, or Semrush's Website Authority Checker. These tools are available directly on their websites, and some offer browser extensions for quick checks. Send your guest post to websites with the most domain authority.

➢ **Link Insertions:** Offer helpful resources or updates to websites already covering your topic.

Quality always outweighs quantity. One backlink from a respected industry leader is worth more than fifty from random blogs.

Real-World Experience & Expertise

Authority isn't just about content volume — it's about *proof of experience.*

That's the "E" in E-E-A-T: **Experience, Expertise, Authoritativeness, and Trustworthiness.**

Anyone can write an article about leadership or cybersecurity. But only someone who's led a team through a crisis or secured networks under pressure can write from the inside out.

Tell the story behind the lesson.

Share what went wrong and how you fixed it.

Include numbers, metrics, or timelines.

Add real photos when possible (AI loves authenticity).

Authentic experience cuts through the noise. When you tell the truth about what you've learned in the field, your readers feel it — and AI models learn to associate your name with expertise in that area.

E-E-A-T and Authority in Practice

E-E-A-T isn't just a Google acronym. It's the universal checklist for credibility in the AI era.

Experience — Have you personally done the thing you're teaching?

Expertise — Are you clearly knowledgeable and precise in your advice?

Authoritativeness — Do other people cite or mention you?

Trustworthiness — Does your online presence feel real, verified, and honest?

To demonstrate these:

> ➤ Sign your work with your real name and credentials.

> ➤ Include a short author bio with relevant background.

> ➤ Show contact information, not just anonymous forms.

> ➤ Be transparent about sources, partners, and limitations.

AI's definition of authority mirrors humanity's: **experience plus integrity, proven over time.**

The Four Pillars of Niche Authority

Depth of Expertise	Consistency of Presence	Social Proof & Citations	Thought Leadership
Become the undeniable expert in your clearly defined domain	Show up everywhere your audience and AI expects to find you	Let others validate your authority	Lead the conversation, don't just join it

Networking and Exposure

Authority expands through networks. Build bridges across multiple online platforms — each serves a unique purpose:

Reddit: One of the most cited sources in AI training data. Participate genuinely. Never self-promote. Contribute thoughtful answers to threads in your niche. A good start is to use **GummySearch** to find Reddit discussions relevant to your industry.

Quora: Create an account to study the questions your customers are asking. Write detailed, useful answers that demonstrate knowledge — not marketing.

LinkedIn: Build professional credibility. Share insights, comment intelligently, and tag peers or partners.

Wikipedia & Wikidata: Create or update your entry if you qualify. Add citations from reliable third-party sources. This improves your digital reputation across AI platforms.

Online authority is strengthened by **visibility + value + verifiability.**

Social Media Credibility & Exposure

Each social platform serves a different purpose — but here's the key: **pick the one where your audience spends time**, not the one you like most.

You might prefer YouTube, but if your customers are on LinkedIn, go there. If your buyers are scrolling Facebook, meet them there.

> ➤ **TikTok:** Primarily for entertainment and quick tips. *Be visual, short, and relatable.*
> ➤ **YouTube:** Best for education and tutorials. *Create value-rich videos that teach something practical.*
> ➤ **LinkedIn:** Focused on professional credibility. *Publish insights, case studies, and leadership content.*
> ➤ **Facebook:** Used for community engagement. *Share updates and connect with local audiences.*
> ➤ **Instagram:** Centered on visual storytelling. *Show behind-the-scenes authenticity.*

> **X (Twitter):** Great for industry commentary. *Add intelligent takes, not noise.*
> **Quora:** Designed for public Q & A. *Give genuine, helpful answers without selling.*
> **Reddit:** Built around discussion and advice. *Provide real help, even anonymously if needed.*
> **Pinterest:** Ideal for visual planning. *Use infographics, checklists, and visual guides.*
> **Medium / Substack:** Geared toward long-form writing. *Publish essays, thought leadership, or deep insights.*

Pro Tip Checklist – Niche Authority

Niche Authority is about being recognized as the go-to expert in your field — not because you say so, but because the internet can prove it.

AI systems reward professionals who show consistent expertise, verified credentials, and authentic engagement within their domain.

To build digital authority, focus on visibility, credibility, and contribution.

✓ **Engage in your niche communities.**

Create an account on Reddit, Quora, or similar platforms and consistently answer real questions in your area of expertise. This builds credibility and creates natural backlinks to your website.

✓ **Register as a verified expert.**

Join journalist and expert platforms such as **Sources of Sources, Help a Reporter Out (HARO)**, and **Featured.com**. These services connect experts with journalists and publications, helping you earn media mentions and authoritative backlinks.

✓ **Write for external websites.**

Contribute guest posts or industry articles on reputable blogs and professional news sites. Choose outlets that your target audience already trusts and that align closely with your brand's niche.

✓ **Get listed in directories and associations.**

Register your business or professional name in local directories, chambers of commerce, and official industry associations. These citations reinforce legitimacy in both human and AI evaluations.

✓ **Collect authentic customer reviews.**

Request reviews that highlight measurable outcomes or transformations. Genuine feedback — not fluff — is one of the strongest indicators of authority.

✓ **Publish a case study.**

Document one real project or client success story with data, quotes, and outcomes. Case studies prove that your methods work in the real world.

✓ **Share professional insights on LinkedIn.**

Post short lessons learned, leadership reflections, or industry updates on your LinkedIn profile, and link them back to your main website or cornerstone content.

✓ **Add yourself to Wikidata (and Wikipedia if eligible).**

Wikidata is one of the primary knowledge sources AI systems use to verify entity relationships. Maintain a factual, neutral profile about your brand or professional background.

✓ **Build topic clusters around your core expertise.**

Create a hub of content that demonstrates depth, not breadth. Show that you understand every angle of your subject, linking supporting posts to a main cornerstone article.

✓ **Verify author identity across your digital presence.**

Ensure your author name, credentials, and contact information are accurate and consistent on every website, social profile, and article you control.

AI Search Prompts – Niche Authority

Below are the AI Search Prompts you can use to help AI strengthen your authority signals and online reputation. These prompts are designed to build visibility, backlinks, and professional recognition within your niche.

➤ "Where does my target audience spend time online, and which social platforms do they use most?"

➤ "Write a guest post pitch email for [industry/topic] offering unique insights for their readers."

➤ "Generate a press release highlighting my company's achievements in [field]."

➤ "Suggest 10 Reddit or Quora threads where I can contribute valuable expertise about [topic]."

➤ "Identify the best backlink opportunities for my business type."

➤ "List 10 podcasts or online publications that regularly feature experts in [industry]."

➤ "Write a HARO or Featured.com response to this journalist query: [paste query]."

➤ "Create a neutral Wikidata entry summary for [brand or person]."

➤ "Generate a LinkedIn article outline that showcases my experience in [specialty]."

➤ "List 5 directory or citation sources that strengthen authority for [business type]."

Closing Reflections

In the Special Forces, being a *Quiet Professional* means doing exceptional work without needing to announce it. In the digital age, the same principle applies: earn respect through consistent excellence before the world knows your name.

Authority today isn't claimed — it's detected.

AI, like people, is constantly asking:

"Is this person credible? Consistent? Trusted by others?"

Every review, mention, and appearance you earn becomes a digital echo of that trust.

Keep showing up with precision, humility, and authenticity — and soon, both humans and algorithms will recognize your name before you even enter the room.

Key Takaways

True authority is earned through consistent value, not self-promotion.

Every verified mention, citation, or collaboration strengthens your digital credibility.

Case studies, expert platforms, and authentic reviews are trust signals AI measures.

Authority compounds — the more you give, teach, and contribute, the more your influence expands.

Quiet confidence and real results will always outlast marketing hype.

Now that your authority is established and your reputation is verified across the web, it's time to move to the final stage: **Data-Driven Improvements** — where you'll learn to measure, adapt, and continuously refine your strategy so your visibility compounds over time.

D — Data-Driven Improvements: Measure, Adapt, Scale

The Iteration Loop -

Growth demands continuous refinement. Use analytics to measure with precision, adapt with speed, and commit to the ongoing cycle of improvement.

How One Piece of Data (a Keyword) Changed Everything

When I first launched *Life is a Special Operation*, I had no real search engine strategy. My website had strong credibility and niche authority — real expertise, real value — but in the world of keywords, I was invisible.

That shocked me. Back then, keywords were everything. If you weren't optimizing for them, you didn't exist. So I decided to start small and look at the data.

The first thing I did was check where I ranked. Even though my content was respected by readers, it wasn't being found by search engines. Then something interesting happened with one of my smaller topics: **PACE planning.**

In the Army, we use a PACE plan — *Primary, Alternate, Contingency, and Emergency* — to create redundancy in communications:

> ➤ **Primary:** an encrypted satellite radio.

> ➤ **Alternate:** an encrypted FM radio.

> ➤ **Contingency:** an unencrypted FM channel.

> ➤ **Emergency:** a satellite phone or even a local cell phone.

This layered system ensures that no matter what happens, communication continues.

PACE planning usually applies to communication plans — but it can, and should, be used for any plan where redundancy is essential.

As it turned out, my PACE plan article was getting a lot more views than my other articles. So I revised it, applying many of the best practices covered in our **O – Optimization** and **U – Utility** chapters. I updated the piece with better structure, schema markup, FAQs, internal links, and clear examples. I refined both the storytelling and the technical SEO.

And the data responded.

At first, I started appearing in search results whenever someone looked for "PACE" or "military planning techniques." Then I began showing up in AI-generated answers and summaries. Within months, *Life is a Special Operation* ranked **#1 globally for "PACE plan."**

That small win wasn't just about one keyword — it was proof of concept.

It showed me that data matters, and that systematic improvement works.

If you're not looking at your data, you'll never know which levers to pull. And if you're not improving based on what you see, you'll never rank high in the world of AI SEO.

Why Data Matters

Search and discovery are no longer static. Google, Bing, ChatGPT, and Gemini evolve daily, and their algorithms rely on pattern recognition. The more consistently you measure and refine, the clearer your digital signal becomes.

The winners in AI SEO aren't those who publish the most — they're those who analyze, adapt, and improve faster than everyone else.

Data-Driven Improvements

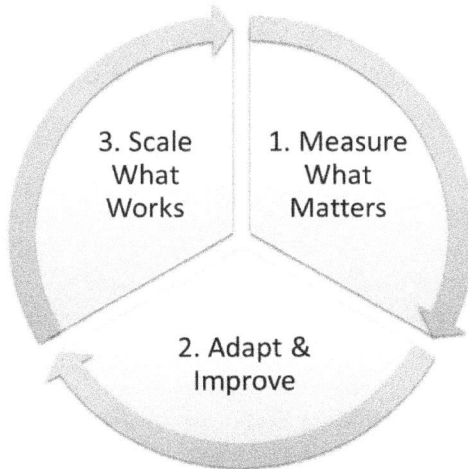

3. Scale What Works

1. Measure What Matters

2. Adapt & Improve

Measure What Matters

There's an ocean of data out there, but only a few currents actually move your business forward.

Track these five categories regularly:

- **Rankings:** Are you visible for your target queries?
- **AI Citations:** How often do AI systems mention or summarize your brand?
- **Reviews:** What are people saying about you — and how frequently?
- **Conversions:** Are visitors taking meaningful action?
- **Engagement:** Do people stay, scroll, comment, and share — or bounce away?

Monitor visibility across AI systems:

- **ChatGPT and Perplexity:** Ask your ideal customer's questions and see if you're cited.
- **Google Gemini / SGE:** Check if your content is included in AI Overviews.
- **Bing Copilot:** Watch for inclusion in summaries or answer cards.

Define new AI-specific KPIs (Key Performance Indicators):

- **AI Citation Share of Voice:** The percentage of AI-generated responses that mention your brand or website in your niche.
- **Answer Box Win Rate:** How often your content earns a featured snippet or AI summary position.
- **Entity Graph Coverage Score:** How completely AI systems understand your business — its name, category, expertise, and reputation.

Data shows reality, not opinion. If you aren't measuring it, you're just guessing.

Diagnose, Adapt, and Improve

Once you gather your data, your job is to translate it into decisions.

Use tools that make feedback fast and actionable:

➢ **Google Search Console:** Track which pages earn impressions and clicks — and which don't.
➢ **Bing Webmaster Tools:** Identify visibility beyond Google.
➢ **Google Analytics / Plausible / Matomo:** Understand how visitors behave and why they convert.
➢ **Screaming Frog:** Crawl your site for broken links, missing titles, or duplicates.
➢ **SurferSEO or Clearscope:** Compare your content's structure and depth against high-ranking competitors.

If a page underperforms, don't panic — diagnose. Check its metadata, internal links, readability, and schema. Then update and re-test.

Improvement is not a single event. It's a cycle — an ongoing conversation between your strategy and your data.

Choose the Right Metrics for You

Every business has its version of "PACE." The key is to find *your* primary, alternate, contingency, and emergency signals — the data points that ensure your communication with the market never breaks down.

Ask yourself:

➢ What metrics actually move my mission forward?
➢ Which data points indicate customer trust and satisfaction?

➢ What negative trends (like unsubscribes or cart abandonments) signal an underlying issue?

Then create a simple dashboard with these categories:

➢ **Visibility** – Rankings, AI mentions, featured snippets
➢ **Engagement** – Read time, clicks, scroll depth
➢ **Conversion** – Form fills, calls, purchases
➢ **Trust** – Reviews, backlinks, social mentions
➢ **Improvement** – Pages optimized, errors fixed, FAQs added

The goal is to look at your digital performance the way you'd monitor a mission — consistently, objectively, and with a bias for action.

Data-Driven Means Continuous Improvements

The word "improvements" is plural for a reason. There's no finish line in SEO or AI visibility. Algorithms change, competitors rise, and customer behavior shifts.

To stay visible, you must commit to a system of **regular measurement and deliberate updates.**

If your company can assign one person full-time to analytics and optimization, do it. If not, assign it as an additional duty — but make it official.

And above all, **put it on the calendar.**

The AI Brand Check — Managing Your Reputation

While this chapter focuses on data — and most people think of data as purely *quantitative* — it's worth remembering that

134

some of the most important insights in business are *qualitative*. Entire PhD dissertations and million-dollar decisions are made every day based on interviews, case studies, and perception analysis.

So before we close this section on Data-Driven Improvements, let's add one more dimension to the discussion: **your professional reputation.**

In the era of generative search, your reputation lives **inside the model.**

When someone asks ChatGPT, Gemini, or Perplexity, *"Who is [Your Name or Brand]?"* the answer they get isn't a simple pull from your website — it's a synthesis of every mention, article, review, and interview connected to you. In other words, AI systems don't quote your About Page; they quote the internet's collective memory of you.

That means you must treat AI like a living public-relations ecosystem. You can't fully control it, but you can deliberately influence it. Start by conducting regular **AI Brand Checks.** Ask major AI platforms what they know about you, your company, your products, and your competitors. Take notes. Are the results accurate, flattering, current, and aligned with your brand message? If not, publish clarifying pieces — FAQs, interviews, case studies, or credible third-party mentions — that correct the record. Every factual, well-structured reference you place online becomes a reinforcement signal that future AI crawlers will use to rebuild your reputation.

You don't need a million followers to shape perception. You just need consistency, credibility, and correction. Make sure the world — and the machines that summarize it — are telling the story you actually want told.

Suggested Rhythm of Review

Weekly

> ➤ Check Google Search Console for indexing errors or new keyword impressions.
> ➤ Read new reviews and respond quickly.
> ➤ Use ChatGPT or Perplexity to test if your brand is appearing in AI-generated results.
> ➤ Watch for traffic spikes or sudden drops.

Monthly

> ➤ Identify top and bottom-performing pages.
> ➤ Track conversion metrics and user behavior patterns.
> ➤ Check backlinks and mentions using Ahrefs, Ubersuggest, or similar tools.
> ➤ Update or republish one key article with better structure or examples.

Quarterly

> ➤ Perform a technical audit (Screaming Frog or Sitebulb).
> ➤ Verify schema accuracy and NAP consistency.
> ➤ Compare this quarter's performance against last quarter's benchmarks.
> ➤ Refine internal linking and topical clusters.

Yearly

> ➤ Conduct a full content audit — merge, refresh, or delete outdated pages.
> ➤ Reassess your keyword and niche authority strategy.
> ➤ Update cornerstone assets (homepage, About, key guides).
> ➤ Publish a case study showing measurable improvement.

Without a schedule, improvement fades into wishful thinking. With one, it becomes predictable progress.

Using AI to Analyze Data

AI tools can now interpret patterns faster than human analysts — but you must give them direction.

Try these workflows:

> ➤ Paste your Google Analytics data into ChatGPT and ask:
> *"What patterns or anomalies stand out?"*
> ➤ Share a CSV of your keywords and ask:
> *"Which ones are trending up or down?"*
> ➤ Combine export files from Search Console and Analytics, then ask:
> *"Which pages bring the most organic conversions?"*

Let AI handle the heavy analysis. Then, as the human strategist, decide what actions matter most.

Turning Data into Action

Every metric should trigger one of three outcomes:

> ➤ **Replicate:** Double down on what works.
> ➤ **Repair:** Fix what's broken or underperforming.
> ➤ **Retire:** Eliminate what's outdated or ineffective.

Each cycle builds strength through refinement. Improvement is a discipline, not a reaction.

The Human Side of Data

There's always temptation to ignore numbers when they don't flatter us. But progress begins the moment you look honestly.

Data isn't personal — it's directional. It tells you where to go next. The businesses that learn fastest are the ones that treat data as a compass, not a critique.

Goal of Data-Driven Improvements

To continuously enhance visibility, trust, and reach through deliberate iteration.

You can't improve what you don't measure — and you can't sustain what you don't review.

Pro Tip Checklist: Data-Driven Improvements

Data-driven improvement means using measurable feedback to guide every decision.

AI SEO success isn't about one-time optimization — it's about disciplined observation, small corrections, and steady progress.

Think of your data as a self-assessment tool — a mirror showing your strengths, blind spots, and the next actions that will move the mission forward.

Weekly Checks

✓ **Review Google Search Console.**

Check for new keyword impressions, coverage issues, and performance drops. Quick responses to these signals prevent long-term losses in visibility.

✓ **Respond to all new customer reviews.**

Acknowledge feedback quickly and professionally. Engagement shows both customers and AI systems that your business is active and attentive.

✓ **Check AI visibility.**

Search your business name and main services in **ChatGPT, Perplexity, and Bing Copilot** to see if your content appears in AI-generated results or summaries.

✓ **Watch for anomalies.**

Use Google Analytics or your preferred dashboard to monitor sudden spikes or dips in traffic, conversions, or engagement.

Monthly Checks

✓ **Identify best and worst performing pages.**

Review which pages bring in the most traffic and which underperform. Optimize or update lagging pages with clearer messaging and stronger calls-to-action.

✓ **Measure conversions and engagement trends.**

Track form fills, downloads, email signups, and user behavior metrics. Identify what content type converts best and replicate its structure.

✓ **Review backlinks and mentions.**

Use tools like **Ahrefs** or **Ubersuggest** to monitor new inbound links, citations, and brand mentions. Strengthen relationships with high-quality referrers.

✓ **Refresh or expand one important article.**

Each month, choose one cornerstone page to improve with updated data, visuals, or FAQs. Incremental content updates compound over time.

Quarterly Checks

✓ **Conduct a technical and structural audit.**

Inspect site speed, security, mobile usability, and internal linking. Resolve any indexing or accessibility issues that slow down performance.

✓ **Verify schema accuracy.**

Run your site through Google's Rich Results Test to ensure all structured data (FAQs, Product, LocalBusiness, etc.) is valid and current.

✓ **Adjust content strategy.**

Base next-quarter priorities on hard numbers — traffic patterns, topic performance, and audience engagement.

✓ **Re-cluster internal links.**

Realign your internal link structure to strengthen your topic clusters and authority pages.

✓ **Treat AI systems like an ongoing reputation audit.**

Once a quarter, ask leading AI platforms to describe your brand in their own words. If they misunderstand you, that's a sign your digital footprint needs reinforcement — not panic, but publication.

Yearly Checks

✓ **Perform a comprehensive content audit.**

Evaluate every page for accuracy, freshness, and alignment with your brand's mission. Remove, merge, or rewrite outdated content.

✓ **Redefine your KPIs and niche goals.**

Adjust your success metrics to reflect where your business and industry are heading.

✓ **Refresh cornerstone content.**

Your flagship guides, services, or "pillar" pages should be updated annually with new data, insights, and visuals.

✓ **Publish one success story or case study.**

Document measurable results from your past year's work. Case studies serve as proof of performance for both clients and AI systems evaluating authority.

AI Search Prompts: Data-Driven Improvements

Below are the AI Search Prompts you can use to help AI analyze, monitor, and improve your digital performance over time.

These prompts align directly with the Pro Tips above and support continuous optimization.

➤ "What are the top 10 performance metrics for [industry type] websites?"

➤ "Summarize key insights from this analytics report: [paste data]."

➤ "Generate a quarterly SEO improvement plan based on these trends."

➤ "Which keywords in this list are gaining momentum?"

➤ "Write an action plan for pages with low click-through rates."

➤ "Create a checklist for AI citation tracking and response."

➤ "Suggest 5 automation tools for monitoring traffic, reviews, and brand mentions."

> ➤ "What does ChatGPT, Perplexity, and Gemini currently say about [My Brand Name]? Summarize any inaccuracies, tone issues, or missing details I should correct with new authoritative content."

Closing Reflections

Amazon didn't become the world's most efficient sales machine by guessing.

Every pixel, product placement, and font choice on that website was tested, measured, and refined. They learned that a white background outperformed black, that a friendly sans-serif font encouraged trust, and that displaying "Customers also bought…" generated billions in additional revenue. None of it was luck — it was data.

That's the power of iteration. Data doesn't just inform decisions; it *reveals truth*.

It shows what people actually do, not what we think they'll do.

AI SEO works the same way. You write, you measure, you adjust. Each improvement — no matter how small — compounds into clarity, trust, and authority.

You don't need to be perfect. You just need to be curious, consistent, and willing to improve.

Because success in AI SEO isn't about one big breakthrough. It's about a thousand small, disciplined refinements — the quiet science of getting better every day.

Key Takeaways

Data tells the truth — every time.

Small, consistent improvements outperform massive one-time efforts.

Responding to feedback is a sign of professionalism, not imperfection.

AI SEO rewards consistency, iteration, and clarity over hype.

The teams who measure, adapt, and refine are the ones who win — every single time.

Now that you've mastered **Data-Driven Improvements**, you've completed the full FOUND framework — **Foundations, Optimization, Utility, Niche Authority, and Data** — the core system that ensures you'll always be found by AI search.

You now have the full FOUND system — next, let's turn it into results.

The Path Forward

Where We've Been

For two decades, SEO meant algorithms, keywords, backlinks, and the endless chase for page-one rankings. Then came the shockwave — AI-driven search. Suddenly the rules changed, and so did the vocabulary.

Some call it **AI SEO**, others **AEO** or **GEO**, and a few even say **LLM SEO** or **Semantic Optimization**. All describe the same shift: search is no longer a list of links — it's a conversation powered by language models.

The final name doesn't matter. What matters is understanding how these systems think and learning to speak their language.

Traditional SEO rewarded keyword tricks; AI SEO rewards clarity, credibility, and meaning. It ranks the most complete and trustworthy answers — not the loudest voices.

Whatever you call it, the goal is the same: **be found by AI search so you can reach more clients and make more money.** The terminology will evolve, but the mission won't.

At its core, AI search works through patterns and probabilities. Large Language Models (LLMs) read, compare, and synthesize trillions of words, building vast "entity graphs" that connect people, businesses, topics, and expertise. When a user asks a question — "What's the best plumber in Boise?" or "How can I build a PACE plan for my company?" — the model predicts which sources seem most trustworthy, complete, and contextually accurate. It doesn't just look for keywords; it looks for signals of authority and coherence.

That shift — from keywords to knowledge — is the great disruption of our time.

Yet not everything changed. The same fundamentals that mattered in classic SEO still matter today: clarity, credibility, structure, and service. Search engines, whether algorithmic or generative, still reward sites that are fast, secure, accessible, and easy to read. The difference is that the audience now includes both humans and machines — and you must communicate effectively with both.

That realization led us to the **FOUND Framework**: a simple, disciplined system for staying visible in an unpredictable landscape. FOUND is the bridge between what used to work and what will always work.

We began with **Foundations** — the idea that your online identity must be consistent, verified, and unmistakable. Then we moved to **Optimization**, learning to translate human expertise into a structure that machines can interpret. **Utility** reminded us that every click is a cry for help, and the only lasting strategy is to be the most helpful answer. **Niche Authority** showed that credibility is earned, not claimed — that the quiet professional who demonstrates mastery through results outlasts the self-promoter every time. And **Data-Driven Improvements** taught us that growth isn't magic; it's measurement applied with discipline.

If the first half of this book was theory, the FOUND Framework was execution — the operational plan that turns knowledge into performance.

Together, these ideas answer the two questions every business owner quietly asks:

How do I stay relevant when technology keeps changing?

How do I make sure people — and AI — know I exist?

The answer is **FOUND**.

When your foundation is solid, your optimization precise, your content genuinely useful, your authority authentic, and your improvements continual, you become algorithm-proof. You stop chasing trends and start compounding trust.

That's where we've been — and why it matters.

Lessons from the FOUND Framework

Each stage of FOUND builds upon the last like a sequence of missions, each one reinforcing the next.

Foundation: Build an Unshakable Digital Presence

Everything starts with ownership and consistency. Your digital identity — your domain, listings, and message — must align perfectly across every platform. The internet rewards unity; confusion kills credibility. When every profile tells the same story, AI recognizes you as one coherent entity. Humans sense it too. *Be clear, be legitimate, be consistent.* That's how trust is earned.

Optimization: Make Your Message Machine-Readable

Optimization isn't about tricking machines — it's about teaching them. Metadata, schema, speed, mobile design, and internal linking aren't vanity metrics; they're the grammar of discoverability. When your structure mirrors your substance, your message travels farther. Machines understand you, humans enjoy you, and trust deepens with every clear signal.

Utility: Create Content That Solves Human Problems

True usefulness begins with a good product or service. No amount of SEO can save mediocrity. If your work is weak, the internet will expose it. But if you genuinely help people — through tutorials, FAQs, checklists, calculators, and honest writing — you'll create gravity. AI detects helpfulness the same way humans do: through clarity, completeness, and empathy. *Help first; visibility follows.*

Niche Authority: Establish Unquestionable Expertise

Authority is not loud. It's steady, proven, and verifiable. Like the quiet professional whose uniform silently tells his story, your expertise shows through consistent results, customer praise, and authentic contributions. Mentions, citations, and backlinks are the digital ribbons of valor — they confirm that others vouch for your skill. When your name carries weight in your field, AI takes notice, because authority leaves a traceable footprint.

Data-Driven Improvements: Measure, Adapt, Scale

The final stage transforms motion into progress. Without data, effort drifts. Tracking rankings, AI citations, reviews, and engagement turn guesswork into intelligence. Improvement isn't a single breakthrough; it's hundreds of micro-adjustments guided by numbers. Review weekly, refine monthly, and audit yearly. Data doesn't criticize — it directs. The organizations that listen to their data move from reactive to unstoppable.

FOUND is more than a checklist — it's a mindset. It teaches you to think like a strategist, write like a teacher, and operate like a professional. Each phase sharpens the next, creating a cycle of clarity, credibility, and growth that feeds itself.

Preparing for the Future of AI SEO

The landscape ahead is vast and volatile. Search is no longer limited to the screen in your hand; it's becoming ambient — woven into every device, platform, and experience. In the coming years, discovery will be **multi-modal** and **context-aware**. People will search with their voices, cameras, and even conversations carried out by digital agents acting on their behalf.

That means your online presence must evolve from being text-optimized to being *experience-optimized*.

AI systems will parse your photos, understand your tone in videos, and read your transcripts to learn what kind of expert you are. They'll map how consistently your identity appears across podcasts, articles, social posts, and metadata. Your brand won't just be read — it will be *understood holistically*.

To prepare, start expanding your definition of content. A blog post is valuable, but so is a short video that demonstrates a process, a podcast episode that explains a principle, or an infographic that simplifies complexity. When you publish in multiple formats — text, audio, video, visual — you create a network of signals that reinforce your expertise across media types.

AI doesn't just see words; it sees relationships. It connects your website to your LinkedIn profile, your YouTube channel to your transcripts, your podcast show notes to your business listing. Every piece of structured information strengthens your position in the digital ecosystem.

How to Future-Proof Your Visibility

- ➤ **Transcribe and Tag Everything.** Upload transcripts for every video and caption every image. Those words become discoverable data.
- ➤ **Standardize Your Metadata.** Use consistent titles, brand names, and descriptions across all media.
- ➤ **Publish Thoughtfully on the Right Platforms.** Don't scatter yourself everywhere; show up where your audience learns.
- ➤ **Collaborate with Credible Voices.** Co-authored content, interviews, and shared projects create entity links that AI uses to assess authority.
- ➤ **Stay Curious.** Experiment with new tools, from visual search to voice optimization, but keep your foundation intact.

Above all, remember that technology rewards the same timeless virtues: clarity, honesty, and usefulness. The interfaces may change; the principles do not.

The future belongs to those who combine technical precision with human warmth — to creators and businesses who prove, through every interaction, that they exist to serve, not to exploit.

2 Toolkits Just for You

Now that you understand the strategy, you need execution tools. The two enclosures that follow are designed to make FOUND actionable.

Enclosure 1: The Consolidated List of Pro Tips condenses all of the Pro Tips within this book into one operational sequence — Foundation → Optimization → Usefulness → Niche Authority → Data. It your perfect cheat sheet. It's your quarterly self-assessment. Use it to confirm alignment and to delegate responsibilities within your team. Think of it as your standard operating procedure for visibility.

Enclosure 2: The Consolidated AI SEO Prompt List turns AI itself into your assistant. These ready-to-use commands for ChatGPT, Gemini, or Perplexity help you generate schema, analyze metrics, draft listings, or audit content without guesswork. Each prompt mirrors the principles in this book — structured, clear, and outcome-driven — so you can scale your expertise without sacrificing authenticity.

Together, these two tools form the bridge from *knowing* to *doing*. They're what keep FOUND alive long after you close this book.

Final Reflection

There are two paths every business can take online.

One spirals downward — the shortcut path. It's filled with clickbait, copied text, fake reviews, and hollow promises. It might spike quickly, but it collapses just as fast. AI recognizes emptiness. So do humans. Once your reputation tilts negative, every algorithm amplifies the decline.

The other path spirals upward — the path of usefulness and integrity. It begins with a good product, honest communication, and respect for the reader's time. When you publish material that genuinely helps, when your words match your actions, the algorithms learn to trust you. People do too. Each positive interaction reinforces the next, and momentum builds.

That's the real power of AI SEO. It doesn't just reward manipulation; it rewards *merit*. The better you serve, the better you're found.

So build something worth finding. Keep your content human, your structure disciplined, and your intent pure. Let data guide you, but let character define you. Over time, that combination becomes unbeatable.

FOUND was never about gaming the system — it's about mastering yourself. It's about bringing professionalism, humility, and excellence into the digital age. When you operate with integrity, your presence compounds. You attract not only customers, but respect.

That's how you rise above the noise.

Be Found by AI Search — and become the best answer.

Enclosure 1: The Consolidated List of Pro Tips

Your Operational Checklist for Being Found by AI Search

How to Use This Checklist

1. **Follow the FOUND sequence** — complete *Foundation → Optimization → Utility → Niche Authority → Data-Driven Improvements* in order.

2. **Revisit quarterly** — algorithms evolve, so your visibility system should too.

3. **Assign ownership** — ensure someone on your team is always responsible for FOUND upkeep.

4. **Track progress** — use a spreadsheet or project board to log updates, audit dates, and metrics.

5. **Treat it like an SOP** — this isn't a campaign; it's your permanent operating system for credibility and discoverability.

Pro Tip Checklist — Foundation

Building your foundation is like setting up your headquarters. If you get this right, everything else — optimization, content, and authority — runs smoother and faster.

Here's how to establish your digital identity step-by-step.

Phase 1: Define Your Business and Brand Mission

Before you build, you must know what you're building for. This is where you define your digital identity — who you are, what you do, and who you serve.

✓ **Decide what your business *is* and what you want to be known for.**

Write a single, clear sentence that describes your service and your promise to customers.

✓ **Define your Ideal Customer Profile (ICP).**

Know exactly who you want to serve. (You'll find a guided prompt later in the book to help define your ICP.)

✓ **Clarify your Unique Value Proposition (UVP).**

What makes your product or service different from competitors? Write it down and use it everywhere.

✓ **Choose your main keywords and topics.**

What should AI and customers associate your business with?

Example: "Emergency Plumbing in Boise" or "Cybersecurity for Small Businesses."

✓ **Select a consistent business name and tagline.**

Use the same name, tagline, and brand language everywhere to reinforce credibility.

✓ **Secure your domain name.**

Purchase your business name (and close variations) using a trusted registrar like HostGator, Google Domains, Namecheap, or GoDaddy.

o   Always use **HTTPS** (secure version).

✓ **Write a short brand mission statement.**

One paragraph explaining what you stand for, who you serve, and why you exist.

o   Keep it in your About page and social media bios.

Phase 2: Register and Verify Your Business Identity

Once you've defined who you are, make sure the internet agrees with you.

✓ **Register your business on all major directories:**

o   **Google Business Profile**
https://www.google.com/business

o   **Bing Places for Business**
https://www.bingplaces.com

o   **Apple Business Connect (Apple Maps)**
https://businessconnect.apple.com

o   **Yelp for Business**
https://biz.yelp.com

o   **LinkedIn Company Page**
https://www.linkedin.com/company/setup/new

o   **Trustpilot**
https://www.trustpilot.com

o   **Better Business Bureau (BBB)**
https://www.bbb.org

o   **Facebook Business Page**
https://www.facebook.com/pages/create

- o **Wikidata Entry**
  https://www.wikidata.org/wiki/Wikidata:Main_Page

- o **Foursquare for Business**
  https://foursquare.com/partners

✓ **Verify each listing.**

Some will send a postcard (Google, Bing), others confirm via email or phone. Verification simply means the address, phone, and email you list actually reach you.

✓ **Maintain consistent NAP (Name – Address – Phone).**

The exact spelling and format must match on every listing. If one says "123 Main St." and another says "123 Main Street," fix it.

✓ **Upload real images.**

Show your team, workspace, and logo. Avoid generic stock photos.

✓ **Create a digital breadcrumb trail.**

Link all your listings and profiles back to your main website — and link your website to those profiles. This interconnected loop confirms that they all belong to the same verified entity — *you*.

Phase 3: Build Trust and Credibility

Trust is the invisible currency of the digital world.

Once your business exists online, show proof that you're real, active, and reputable.

✓ **Set up a review platform (choose one or two).**

- o If you're a local business: **Google Reviews** or **Trustpilot**.

- o Don't overwhelm yourself with too many review sites; consistency beats quantity.

✓ **Develop a simple customer review system.**

After each sale or service, send a short message or QR code link asking for feedback.

✓ **Respond to reviews regularly.**

Acknowledge both praise and criticism — AI recognizes responsiveness as legitimacy.

✓ **List your business hours and contact info clearly.**

Keep them updated on all profiles and your website footer.

✓ **Use the same logo, brand colors, and fonts everywhere.**

Uniform branding equals professional trust.

✓ **Add licenses, certifications, and awards** (if applicable).

These signals strengthen your credibility in both human and machine eyes.

✓ **Show your human side.**

Include short bios, photos, or mission statements about your team. AI values authentic, verifiable entities — not faceless websites.

Phase 4: Maintain, Monitor, and Adapt

The final phase of foundation work isn't glamorous, but it's what separates the amateurs from the pros.

A strong foundation needs regular checks and updates.

✓ **Audit your profiles quarterly.**

Revisit each major listing, directory, and link to ensure they're still accurate.

✓ **Test your website links.**

Make sure all your directory buttons and contact links work. Broken links erode trust.

✓ **Keep your email monitored and phone answered.**

These are digital "heartbeats" — if they go unanswered, you appear inactive.

✓ **Back up your website and data monthly.**

Prevents catastrophic loss if your host or system fails.

✓ **Stay updated on platform policies.**

Google, Yelp, and Facebook update guidelines often. Stay compliant to remain visible.

Pro Tip Checklist — Optimization

Optimization is an ongoing discipline, not a one-time setup.

To make it manageable, I recommend that you break "Optimization" into two categories:

3. **Pro Tips for Your Entire Website** – foundational setup tasks that affect every page.
4. **Pro Tips for Each Page or Blog Article** – repeatable actions for every piece of content you publish.

Each layer strengthens the one before it. Begin with the full-website setup, then move into individual optimization.

Pro Tips for Your Entire Website

✓ **Enable HTTPS (secure connection).**

Confirm that your site loads as **https://** instead of **http://**. Activate a free SSL certificate through your hosting provider or Let's Encrypt, and redirect all non-secure URLs to secure ones.

✓ **Create and submit an XML sitemap.**

Most SEO plugins like Yoast or Rank Math generate this automatically. You can usually find it at *yourdomain.com/sitemap_index. xml*. Submit the sitemap to **Google Search Console** and **Bing Webmaster Tools**.

✓ **Check your robots.txt file.**

Visit *yourdomain.com/robots.txt* to ensure it isn't blocking key pages. A "Disallow: /" line can prevent your entire site from being indexed. Yoast manages this automatically, but it's worth confirming manually.

✓ **Add your business NAP (Name – Address – Phone).**

Include this information in your website footer and on your Contact page. Make sure it matches exactly with your listings on Google, Bing, Apple, and Yelp.

✓ **Activate Core Web Vitals tracking.**

Run a test at **pagespeed.web.dev**. Address any red flags in performance, accessibility, or best practices to improve speed and user experience.

✓ **Design mobile-first.**

Preview your website on multiple phones and tablets. Check that text is readable, buttons are easy to tap, and layout shifts are minimal.

✓ **Enable schema automation.**

Confirm that your SEO plugin (Yoast or Rank Math) has schema enabled by default. If not, plan to add JSON-LD manually later using the provided prompt in this book.

✓ **Secure your brand identity.**

Use the same logo, tagline, and tone of voice across your website and social media channels. Consistency helps AI verify that all your properties belong to the same entity.

✓ **Audit quarterly.**

Every three months, recheck your robots.txt, sitemap, page speed, and schema to ensure nothing has silently broken in the background.

Pro Tips for Each Page or Blog Article

✓ **Set a meta title (under 60 characters).**

Include your main keyword and brand name. Example: *Emergency Plumbing in Boise | Smith Plumbing.*

✓ **Write a meta description (under 160 characters).**

Summarize the page's benefit in plain English. Example: *24/7 Boise plumbers for leaks, clogs, and emergencies.*

✓ **Use a clean URL slug.**

Keep it short, lowercase, and hyphenated. Example: */boise-emergency-plumbing.*

✓ **Include one H1 heading per page.**

Your H1 should clearly describe the topic of the page or article.

✓ **Organize with H2 and H3 subheadings.**

Think of H2s as section headers and H3s as supporting points. They help both humans and AI understand structure.

✓ **Add a TL;DR summary at the top.**

Write two to four sentences summarizing what the page delivers. Both AI systems and readers appreciate a quick overview.

✓ **End with a Key Takeaways box.**

This reinforces clarity and makes your content more likely to appear in AI summaries and snippets.

✓ **Add two to four internal links.**

Connect relevant pages using descriptive anchor text. Example: *Learn more about our water heater services.*

✓ **Optimize every image.**

Rename image files with descriptive keywords (e. g., *boise-water-heater. webp*). Add alt text that explains what's shown in natural language. Example: *Technician installing a new water heater in a Boise home.*

✓ **Add canonical tags to avoid duplicates.**

Yoast handles this automatically, but verify that each page specifies its "official" version.

✓ **Add schema markup.**

Include LocalBusiness, Product, Service, or FAQ schema depending on the page type. Plugin-generated schema works, but custom JSON-LD provides better precision.

✓ **Check page speed before publishing.**

Compress large images, enable caching, and use a performance-friendly host to ensure quick loading.

✓ **Test every page on mobile.**

Use your actual phone, not just a desktop simulator. Verify that everything displays properly without zooming or broken elements.

✓ **Add contact information in the footer.**

This reinforces legitimacy and makes it easy for customers to reach you.

✓ **Verify all internal and external links.**

Fix broken ones and update outdated references once a year.

✓ **FAQs for blog articles:**

Add a short FAQ section with three to eight real customer questions and answers. Mark it up with JSON-LD using your SEO plugin. Include Article and Author schema, refresh content annually with new data, and monitor analytics for engagement and topic relevance.

✓ **Verify that Your Page is Indexed (Visible):**

If your pages aren't appearing in Google results, check Google Search Console. It will often show "Crawled – Not Indexed" or "Blocked by robots.txt," which tells you exactly what's wrong.

Pro Tip Checklist — Utility

✓ **Make it instantly helpful.**

Start with a clear TL;DR summary that gives the main answer up front. Define the reader's problem in plain English, and use numbered steps with short, simple verbs. Add time, cost, or skill-level tags for each step to set expectations, and whenever possible, include a downloadable checklist or worksheet.

✓ **Create multi-layered understanding.**

Add a short Definitions Box for every piece of jargon. Include at least one formula or visual example that explains a key concept, and consider a "myth vs. fact" element to correct common misconceptions. Keep paragraphs short and use white space generously to make your writing feel open and easy to follow.

✓ **Blend empathy with expertise (E-E-A-T: Experience, Expertise, Authoritativeness, and Trustworthiness).**

Add a short "From the Field" note or a relevant photo that illustrates authenticity. Show your face or your voice in at least one format — video, podcast, or author bio — to make your expertise relatable. Mention credentials naturally, not boastfully, and acknowledge what's not included in your guide; transparency builds trust.

✓ **Teach with FAQs and tools.**

Use real questions from your clients or audience emails. Keep each answer under five sentences, and add FAQ schema so AI systems can read and display them accurately. When possible, offer a simple calculator, estimator, or downloadable tool to make your guidance immediately actionable.

✓ **Build depth and storytelling.**

Organize your content into topic clusters that support cornerstone guides. Each major topic should connect to related subtopics, creating a web of understanding. Include at least two content formats (such as video or infographic) for each cornerstone piece, and refresh those main articles annually to keep them current and authoritative.

✓ **Win the Moment, Own the Decade**

Timeliness content creates discovery; timelessness creates authority. Fast content earns mentions, but evergreen content earns memory. Make sure your content calendar includes both — short, reactionary posts that catch AI attention *now*, and long-form, foundational pieces that ensure AI keeps finding you *later*.

Pro Tip Checklist – Niche Authority

Niche Authority is about being recognized as the go-to expert in your field — not because you say so, but because the internet can prove it.

AI systems reward professionals who show consistent expertise, verified credentials, and authentic engagement within their domain.

To build digital authority, focus on visibility, credibility, and contribution.

✓ **Engage in your niche communities.**

Create an account on Reddit, Quora, or similar platforms and consistently answer real questions in your area of expertise. This builds credibility and creates natural backlinks to your website.

✓ **Register as a verified expert.**

Join journalist and expert platforms such as **Sources of Sources, Help a Reporter Out (HARO)**, and **Featured.com**. These services connect experts with journalists and publications, helping you earn media mentions and authoritative backlinks.

✓ **Write for external websites.**

Contribute guest posts or industry articles on reputable blogs and professional news sites. Choose outlets that your target audience already trusts and that align closely with your brand's niche.

✓ **Get listed in directories and associations.**

Register your business or professional name in local directories, chambers of commerce, and official industry associations. These citations reinforce legitimacy in both human and AI evaluations.

✓ **Collect authentic customer reviews.**

Request reviews that highlight measurable outcomes or transformations. Genuine feedback — not fluff — is one of the strongest indicators of authority.

✓ **Publish a case study.**

Document one real project or client success story with data, quotes, and outcomes. Case studies prove that your methods work in the real world.

✓ **Share professional insights on LinkedIn.**

Post short lessons learned, leadership reflections, or industry updates on your LinkedIn profile, and link them back to your main website or cornerstone content.

✓ **Add yourself to Wikidata (and Wikipedia if eligible).**

Wikidata is one of the primary knowledge sources AI systems use to verify entity relationships. Maintain a factual, neutral profile about your brand or professional background.

✓ **Build topic clusters around your core expertise.**

Create a hub of content that demonstrates depth, not breadth. Show that you understand every angle of your subject, linking supporting posts to a main cornerstone article.

✓ **Verify author identity across your digital presence.**

Ensure your author name, credentials, and contact information are accurate and consistent on every website, social profile, and article you control.

Pro Tip Checklist: Data-Driven Improvements

Data-driven improvement means using measurable feedback to guide every decision.

AI SEO success isn't about one-time optimization — it's about disciplined observation, small corrections, and steady progress.

Think of your data like reconnaissance: it tells you where you're winning, where you're exposed, and what to adjust next.

Weekly Checks

✓ **Review Google Search Console.**

Check for new keyword impressions, coverage issues, and performance drops. Quick responses to these signals prevent long-term losses in visibility.

✓ **Respond to all new customer reviews.**

Acknowledge feedback quickly and professionally. Engagement shows both customers and AI systems that your business is active and attentive.

✓ **Check AI visibility.**

Search your business name and main services in **ChatGPT, Perplexity, and Bing Copilot** to see if your content appears in AI-generated results or summaries.

✓ **Watch for anomalies.**

Use Google Analytics or your preferred dashboard to monitor sudden spikes or dips in traffic, conversions, or engagement.

Monthly Checks

✓ **Identify best and worst performing pages.**

Review which pages bring in the most traffic and which underperform. Optimize or update lagging pages with clearer messaging and stronger calls-to-action.

✓ **Measure conversions and engagement trends.**

Track form fills, downloads, email signups, and user behavior metrics. Identify what content type converts best and replicate its structure.

✓ **Review backlinks and mentions.**

Use tools like **Ahrefs** or **Ubersuggest** to monitor new inbound links, citations, and brand mentions. Strengthen relationships with high-quality referrers.

✓ **Refresh or expand one important article.**

Each month, choose one cornerstone page to improve with updated data, visuals, or FAQs. Incremental content updates compound over time.

Quarterly Checks

✓ **Conduct a technical and structural audit.**

Inspect site speed, security, mobile usability, and internal linking. Resolve any indexing or accessibility issues that slow down performance.

✓ **Verify schema accuracy.**

Run your site through Google's Rich Results Test to ensure all structured data (FAQ, Product, Local Business, etc.) is valid and current.

✓ **Adjust content strategy.**

Base next-quarter priorities on hard numbers — traffic patterns, topic performance, and audience engagement.

✓ **Re-cluster internal links.**

Realign your internal link structure to strengthen your topic clusters and authority pages.

✓ **Treat AI systems like an ongoing reputation audit.**

Once a quarter, ask leading AI platforms to describe your brand in their own words. If they misunderstand you, that's a sign your digital footprint needs reinforcement — not panic, but publication.

Yearly Checks

✓ **Perform a comprehensive content audit.**

Evaluate every page for accuracy, freshness, and alignment with your brand's mission. Remove, merge, or rewrite outdated content.

✓ **Redefine your KPIs and niche goals.**

Adjust your success metrics to reflect where your business and industry are heading.

✓ **Refresh cornerstone content.**

Your flagship guides, services, or "pillar" pages should be updated annually with new data, insights, and visuals.

✓ **Publish one success story or case study.**

Document measurable results from your past year's work. Case studies serve as proof of performance for both clients and AI systems evaluating authority.

Enclosure 2: The Consolidated AI SEO Prompt List

Your Complete Prompt System for Implementing the FOUND Framework

The prompt list is your operational playbook for applying the **FOUND Framework** — *Foundations, Optimization, Utility, Niche Authority, and Data-Driven Improvements* — directly inside powerful AI tools like **ChatGPT**, **Gemini**, **Perplexity**, and **Bing Copilot**.

These prompts are designed to help small to medium-sized businesses **be found by AI search** and **become the most helpful, trusted answer** in their industry.

Each prompt mirrors the real-world tasks covered throughout this book and converts those strategies into practical, ready-to-use AI commands.

If you're reading this in the **paperback or hardcover edition**, you can download a free, fully formatted **digital copy** of the Consolidated AI SEO Prompt List at:

☞ **FoundByAISearch.com/prompts**

How to Use the AI SEO Prompt List

1. **Copy the relevant prompt** directly into your preferred AI tool (ChatGPT, Gemini, Perplexity, or Bing Copilot).
2. **Customize the prompt** by adding your own brand name, URLs, niche, or specific business context inside the [brackets].
3. **Run the prompt** and review the AI's response for accuracy, clarity, and tone — remember, *you are still the expert in the loop.*
4. **Edit or refine** the prompt wording if needed until the results meet your expectations.
5. **Save what works** into your team's SOPs, content workflows, or automation systems so you can repeat and scale your success.

How This Section Is Organized

Below you'll find **the complete list of AI Search Master Prompts**, numbered **1 through N** for easy reference. Each prompt corresponds to one phase of the **FOUND Framework**:

- ➤ **F — Foundation:** Build an Unshakable Digital Presence
- ➤ **O — Optimization:** Make Your Message Machine-Readable
- ➤ **U — Utility:** Create Content That Solves Human Problems
- ➤ **N — Niche Authority:** Establish Unquestionable Expertise
- ➤ **D — Data-Driven Improvements:** Measure, Adapt, Scale

After the numbered list, you'll find **an expanded guide** explaining *how to write and adapt each prompt* for your business.

This section turns every prompt into a tool — showing you what to include, why it works, and how to modify it for maximum impact.

AI Search Prompts — Foundation

Below are the AI Search Prompts you can use to help AI strengthen your business foundation. Most of these prompts correspond directly with the Pro Tips, while a few (such as "register your business with the Better Business Bureau") are simple action steps that don't require a prompt.

Phase 1: Define Your Business and Brand Mission

➢ "Help me define my Ideal Customer Profile (ICP) based on my business description: [paste description]."

➢ "Write a one-sentence summary of what my business does and who it serves."

➢ "Suggest a unique value proposition that differentiates my business from competitors."

➢ "List five tagline ideas based on this mission: [paste mission]."

➢ "Recommend keyword-rich but natural domain names for my business idea."

➢ "What are 10 keyword phrases AI systems might associate with my business type?"

Phase 2: Register and Verify Your Business Identity

➢ "Which directories matter most for my specific industry?"

➢ "Should I register on both Trustpilot and Google Reviews, or focus on one?"

➤ "What information should my Google Business Profile include for maximum AI impact?"

➤ "Check this NAP for consistency: [paste business name, address, phone]."

➤ "Generate a 75-word business description with my primary keyword."

Phase 3: Build Trust and Credibility

➤ "Write a customer follow-up message asking politely for a Google or Trustpilot review."

➤ "Suggest five ways to humanize my brand online without showing my face."

➤ "List professional certifications or associations that would build credibility in [industry]."

➤ "Draft a 100-word 'About Us' paragraph including location and service keywords."

➤ "How should I respond professionally to a negative online review?"

Phase 4: Maintain, Monitor, and Adapt

➤ "Create a quarterly digital audit checklist for my business listings and website."

➤ "Suggest tools to alert me if my business name or reviews change online."

➤ "Generate a 12-month reminder calendar for content, reviews, and audits."

➤ "Write a short SOP for updating my business listings."

> ➤ "Recommend automation tools to monitor broken links or downtime."

AI Search Prompts — Optimization

Below are the AI Search Prompts you can use to help AI optimize your website and content for machine understanding.

Website-Wide Prompts

> ➤ "Analyze my website's Core Web Vitals and suggest 5 improvements."
> ➤ "Check my robots.txt and sitemap structure for SEO issues."
> ➤ "Generate JSON-LD schema for my business type: [describe business]."
> ➤ "Suggest ways to improve mobile readability for my homepage."
> ➤ "Audit my site branding for consistency across all pages."

Page & Blog Prompts

> ➤ "Write a meta title and description for this page: [paste text]."
> ➤ "Generate a TL;DR summary and three Key Takeaways for this article."
> ➤ "Suggest internal linking opportunities between these pages: [list URLs]."
> ➤ "Write FAQ schema with 5 questions and answers about [topic]."
> ➤ "Optimize alt text for the following images: [describe or list filenames]."
> ➤ "Generate canonical tags and schema recommendations for this page."

AI Search Prompts — Utility

Below are the AI Search Prompts you can use to help AI make your content more useful, human-centered, and complete. Most of these prompts correspond directly with the Pro Tips, while a few focus on tone and storytelling.

- ➢ "Convert this article into a human-help guide with a TL;DR, problem statement, 7-step process, Definitions box, FAQ (5 Q & As), and a clear call-to-action."

- ➢ "Write a Definitions & Formulas box for [topic]. Include 5 terms, 1 formula, and 1 real-world example."

- ➢ "Generate 6 realistic FAQs for [service]. Keep answers conversational and under 80 words."

- ➢ "Create a 1-page checklist (PDF-ready) mirroring this 7-step process."

- ➢ "Propose a simple calculator idea (inputs, formula, output) for this page."

- ➢ "Rewrite this article in an empathetic, conversational tone that sounds human and authentic."

- ➢ "Suggest two alternate content formats (video or audio) to repurpose this post."

- ➢ "Add a short 'From the Field' paragraph to illustrate experience and credibility."

- ➢ "Write a short post reacting to today's [industry event/news] that explains what it means for [my target audience]. Use clear, factual language so AI systems can cite it accurately."

AI Search Prompts – Niche Authority

Below are the AI Search Prompts you can use to help AI strengthen your authority signals and online reputation.

These prompts are designed to build visibility, backlinks, and professional recognition within your niche.

- ➤ "Where does my target audience spend time online, and which social platforms do they use most?"

- ➤ "Write a guest post pitch email for [industry/topic] offering unique insights for their readers."

- ➤ "Generate a press release highlighting my company's achievements in [field]."

- ➤ "Suggest 10 Reddit or Quora threads where I can contribute valuable expertise about [topic]."

- ➤ "Identify the best backlink opportunities for my business type."

- ➤ "List 10 podcasts or online publications that regularly feature experts in [industry]."

- ➤ "Write a HARO or Featured.com response to this journalist query: [paste query]."

- ➤ "Create a neutral Wikidata entry summary for [brand or person]."

- ➤ "Generate a LinkedIn article outline that showcases my experience in [specialty]."

- ➤ "List 5 directory or citation sources that strengthen authority for [business type]."

AI Search Prompts: Data-Driven Improvements

Below are the AI Search Prompts you can use to help AI analyze, monitor, and improve your digital performance over time.

These prompts align directly with the Pro Tips above and support continuous optimization.

➤ "What are the top 10 performance metrics for [industry type] websites?"

➤ "Summarize key insights from this analytics report: [paste data]."

➤ "Generate a quarterly SEO improvement plan based on these trends."

➤ "Which keywords in this list are gaining momentum?"

➤ "Write an action plan for pages with low click-through rates."

➤ "Create a checklist for AI citation tracking and response."

➤ "Suggest 5 automation tools for monitoring traffic, reviews, and brand mentions."

➤ "What does ChatGPT, Perplexity, and Gemini currently say about [My Brand Name]? Summarize any inaccuracies, tone issues, or missing details I should correct with new authoritative content."

Final Chapter — Do You Need More?

You've reached the end of *AI SEO 2026*.

If you've made it this far, you're already ahead of most business owners — the ones who still haven't realized that AI has changed the way people find, trust, and choose who they do business with.

Now, you understand the **FOUND Framework** — the foundation for visibility in the age of AI Search:

F — Foundation: Build an unshakable digital presence.

O — Optimization: Make your message machine-readable.

U — Utility: Create content that solves human problems.

N — Niche Authority: Establish unquestionable expertise.

D — Data-Driven Improvements: Measure, adapt, and scale.

You've also collected dozens of **Pro Tips** and **Prompts** throughout this book — practical tools that can start improving your visibility right now.

But information alone doesn't create results. Action does. If you're ready to move from *learning* to *doing*, here are your next steps.

Option 1: The Master Visibility Plan (MVP) — Checklist

If you're ready to take charge and implement everything you've learned, the **Master Visibility Plan (MVP)** is your next move.

The MVP Checklist is the *do-it-yourself* implementation system built directly from this book. It organizes all of the **Pro Tips**, **Prompts**, and **FOUND Framework steps** into one clear, step-by-step plan.

This downloadable PDF gives you a complete blueprint for improving your online visibility — with no guesswork, no coding, and no confusion. Whether you're a small business owner or part of a marketing team, you'll know exactly what to do next to make your business discoverable, trustworthy, and findable by AI Search.

Here's what makes it powerful:

➢ **Anybody can do it** – A 50-minute checklist replaces 50 hours of confusion. No jargon. No complexity.

➢ **Be found** – Every task is built on the proven **FOUND Framework** from *AI SEO 2026*, designed to help AI systems like ChatGPT, Gemini, and Bing recognize and recommend your business.

➢ **Act now** – AI search adoption is accelerating. The businesses that adapt today will dominate tomorrow.

➢ **Everything in one place** – Every **Pro Tip, Prompt,** and **FOUND action step** organized into one reusable, downloadable checklist.

➢ **Built by a trusted team** – Developed by the FoundByAISearch.com experts, this checklist distills proven strategies and real-world results into a simple, step-by-step system that ensures your business is found by AI.

- ➢ **Confidence** – Download now and start building visibility before your competitors do.

- ➢ **Risk-free** – One-time purchase. No subscriptions, no upsells, no hidden costs — and a **14-day Money-Back Guarantee.**

You can download the **Master Visibility Plan (MVP) — Checklist** at:

https://foundbyaisearch.com/product/master-visibility-plan/

It's the fastest way to move from *knowing* what to do — to *actually doing it.*

Option 2: The Visibility Index Profile (VIP) — Audit

If you'd rather have a professional handle the analysis for you, the **Visibility Index Profile (VIP)** Audit is the "done-for-you" version of the MVP.

Our expert team will personally evaluate your website through every stage of the **FOUND Framework**, identify your strengths and opportunities, and deliver a **customized Visibility Index Report** with clear, prioritized recommendations for improvement.

You'll begin by completing a short intake form with your business details — your industry, website, and top products or services. Then, within just **two business days**, we'll deliver your tailored audit: a detailed, data-backed report showing how to make your business more discoverable and trusted by AI Search systems like ChatGPT, Gemini, Bing, and Perplexity.

Here's what makes the VIP Audit different:

➤ **Clarity without confusion** – See exactly where your site stands today and what AI sees when it scans your brand.

➤ **Done for you** – You don't lift a finger. Our team runs every test, evaluates your site, and compiles your report.

➤ **Prioritized roadmap** – Receive a custom visibility plan showing what to fix, in what order, and why it matters.

➤ **Expert-built –** Created by the FoundByAISearch.com team, this audit combines professional precision with data-driven strategy to deliver actionable insights that work.

➤ **Immediate results** – Clients receive their completed report within **2 business days.**

➤ **One-time price** – No contracts, no subscriptions, no upsells — just a powerful audit and a clear plan for success.

➤ **14-Day Money-Back Guarantee** – If you're not completely satisfied with the clarity and value of your report, we'll make it right.

You can schedule your **Visibility Index Profile (VIP) — Audit** here:

https://foundbyaisearch.com/product/visibility-index-profile/

For business owners who want certainty instead of trial-and-error, this is the easy button — clarity, confidence, and a personalized path to visibility.

Together, the **MVP Checklist** and **VIP Audit** form the bridge between *understanding* and *implementation*.

Whether you prefer to execute the checklist yourself or have our team perform the audit for you, both paths lead to the same goal: to make your business the most **findable, credible, and trusted** option in the era of AI Search.

A Closing Thought

AI Search isn't on the horizon — it's already here.

Every day, millions of potential customers are asking AI systems questions your business could be answering. You now have the mindset, the framework, and the tools to make that happen.

Thank you for reading *AI SEO 2026* and for investing the time to prepare your business for the future. My mission in writing this book was simple: to help entrepreneurs and small businesses stay ahead of technological change — not get left behind by it.

I hope this book has given you clarity, confidence, and direction.

Now it's time to take the next step —
to be found by AI Search,
so you can get more clients, and make more money.

www.ingramcontent.com/pod-product-compliance
Lightning Source LLC
Chambersburg PA
CBHW031854200326
41597CB00012B/401